THE NATIONAL TRUST
GARDENING GUIDES

BORDERS

PENELOPE HOBHOUSE

THE NATIONAL TRUST
GARDENING GUIDES

BORDERS

PENELOPE HOBHOUSE

SERIES EDITOR
PENELOPE HOBHOUSE

PAVILION
MICHAEL JOSEPH

Published in association with
THE NATIONAL TRUST
36 Queen Anne's Gate
London SW1H 9AS

First published in Great Britain in 1989 by
PAVILION BOOKS LIMITED
196 Shaftesbury Avenue, London WC2H 8JL
in association with Michael Joseph Limited
27 Wrights Lane, Kensington, W8 5TZ

Designed by Bridgewater Design

A CIP catalogue record for this book is
available from the British Library

ISBN 1 85145 237 0

Printed and bound by Mohndruck, West Germany

10 9 8 7 6 5 4 3 2 1

PUBLISHER'S NOTE

Unlike botanical names, the common names for plants are
governed by no international rules. For this gardening
series we have adopted The National Trust style which is
to use initial capitals for common names referring to a single
species. Where the name consists of two or more words, the
first letter of each word is capitalised. General names which
refer to a number of species are not capitalised. All common
names are printed in roman.

CONTENTS

INTRODUCTION

The charm of 'English' flower gardening lies partly in the mixture of styles which are used in making the decorative borders. These styles are distinguished by the type of plants which are found growing in them. Chapters in this book describe border planning for each of the main plant categories. The traditional **herbaceous border** of Chapter 1 belongs to the purist; only hardy perennials are planted for a flowering peak in mid- and late summer. There are modifications of this theme; plants can be chosen for their foliage contribution as well as their usually more fleeting flower power, and bulbs (including corms and rhizomes) and annuals can be planted in drifts between the clumps of sturdy perennials. This sort of border, with soil well prepared and enriched before planting, can be superb in one season – probably 'peaking' the third summer – and needing revision during succeeding seasons.

At the opposite extreme is the labour-saving **shrub border** (see Chapter 2) composed only of woody subjects, which takes some years to achieve its effects; in it flowers and foliage are important but so too is form and habit. The shrub border has a more decidedly architectural composition and a more definite three-dimensional quality which lasts through the whole year rather than only the summer months. Shrub beds can be designed so that ultimately no soil is visible between the plants; alternatively low-growing perennials can be used as an undercarpet to make drifts of attractive flowers or leaf-cover beneath and between the shrub canopies. Spring bulbs will also thrive beneath the branches of deciduous shrubs. A shrub border, grown to maturity, is very labour-saving, and usually looks its best in spring. Later seasonal effects depend on the shapes and density of individual bushes and the varied colour of leaves.

The third and most commonly adopted style is the **mixed border** (see Chapter 3). Any plants – woody or not, hardy or tender – are used which will make a design beautiful and give a long season of beauty. A cottage-garden style where small trees, shrubs, herbaceous plants and bulbs are skilfully interwoven can achieve more all-the-year-round perfection, but results depend on the amount of effort put into it. There are few rules to be formulated; success depends on constant rearranging and juggling of non-woody plants to maintain an aesthetic (and horticultural) balance with the trees and shrubs.

Above: In the forecourt at Hardwick Hall the mixed planting scheme puts an equal emphasis on flowers and foliage.
Opposite: Backed by a high wall the border at Oxburgh, edged with flowing catmints, is a model example of fine colour planning.

There is a fourth category of border style: borders, like parterres, can be planted entirely with spring- and summer-flowering annuals, autumn-planted for spring flowering or planted in early summer for a succeeding four-month performance. Instead of being massed at uniform heights as in colourful parterres, tall, medium and shorter-growing annuals are composed in drifts and blocks to give the same sort of visual effects as more permanent hardy plants. True annual borders are comparatively rare; but groups of both spring- and summer-flowering annuals are often used as 'infillers' between any more permanent planting. In fact annuals may well play an important part in enriching the appearance of all the different categories of border: the herbaceous, the shrub and the mixed.

Inside each of these 'styles' lie extremes of either formality or casualness. Gardening is so personal that even the implementation of a detailed planting plan will give very different results when organized by different hands. Chapter 4 provides some of the basic methods and information necessary for making and maintaining any successful border.

Defining a 'border'

Traditionally a border edged a lawn or ran along a path and was usually backed by a wall, hedge or espalier fruit, which contributed horizontal and vertical structural lines to the scheme and held the design together. Background walls would be draped with curtains of foliage and flower, contributing to the colour scheme of the foreground planting; dark yew or paler green beech hedging acted as a foil to bright floral hues, while patterns of clipped fruit trees, usually found in a walled kitchen garden, provided a firm architectural element in the garden as well as being attractively utilitarian.

Today we use the term 'border' rather loosely. A border is no longer necessarily the edging to a lawn or pathway; nor is it the grand and tailored affair which became such a

Large groups of strong-growing perennials, supported by invisible netting, flourish in the borders at Crathes Castle.

popular feature in the opulent years of the beginning of this century. Borders today are more likely to be distinguished by a planting style than by a definite location. Practically every modern garden has a 'border' of some kind regardless of its actual position; it is not always a continuous edging as implied by the term, but comprises any densely planted area where plants of different heights are grown. In a modestly sized garden this may be the only flower-bed or patch of decorative planting, the rest of the garden consisting of smooth horizontal expanses of lawn, gravel and paving, with the occasional ornamental tree to give height and complete the design. When it is the only such planting, it has to be decorative for all seasons of the year and in a small garden is usually of 'mixed' style; in a larger garden separate areas can have more specific peak periods and therefore more specific colour schemes or plant types – an example would be an iris bed which (since it becomes tatty after flowering) is visited only when looking its best early in the summer.

In today's smaller gardens traditional border plants are often used in island beds cut out of the lawn or located in a dry paved area. In Victorian times (and earlier) these beds were planted with low-growing massed annuals in colourful geometric patterns to be admired and appreciated as a mosaic, their effects captured in one glance; spring and summer bedding schemes followed each other in monotonous rhythm. Today's more complicated island patterns are viewed from all sides and are for all seasons: at the front of each edge of the bed low-growing plants are backed by taller shrubs or perennials which provide a central spine and screen so that an element of surprise is maintained.

It is the composition of different groups of plants, at different heights, with form, foliage and flower variations, which gives each border its unique character. Borders are three-dimensional, and different planes and masses allow light and shadow to play on flower and foliage while ground-hugging plants contrast with soaring spires of stately neighbours. Each individual border plant has its own qualities (unlike the annuals, which are best in carpets of uniform height) and groups are put together so that a balanced pictorial composition results – an artistic masterpiece as well as a convincing demonstration of horticultural skills.

Regardless of which type of plant is used to make up a border scheme it is how plants are arranged from an aesthetic point of view which finally determines results.

The most skilled horticulturist can give plants all their requirements for thriving but fail to achieve any artistic balance and beauty. Borders of all these 'types' can have orchestrated colour schemes; sometimes these are very strict, with definite repetition of colour blocks to make a recognizable pattern: at other times colours in harmony or contrast are woven together to give a more impressionistic atmosphere. How this is done makes all the difference. A well-put-together border gives the effect of a single pictorial composition or a series of different compositions to be viewed from different angles and in different

In the Walled Garden at Penrhyn Castle box-edged beds are massed with brightly-coloured petunias and fuchsias; silver-leaved Stachys *lines a bed of scarlet roses.*

At Overbecks, in the favoured microclimate, semi-tropical plants give variety in the mixed borders.

and proportion; flowering time can vary each year, and plants react to weather variations in different ways. The gardener making a border needs not only the skilled eye of a painter to plan the composition but also all the horticultural knowledge possible to ensure that the results are as predicted.

However formal the planting is in any of these different types of border, sometimes with a repetition of plant groups and colours, it still remains a much more complicated form of gardening than massing annuals in concentric circles or other appropriate patterns. The latter involves following a series of rules of design; attractive parterre patterns are easily achieved if the plant material to implement them is readily available and the soil is regularly dug and enriched.

seasons. The success of a scheme obviously does not depend only on a succession of flower colour; each plant will flower in its turn for only a limited period. The picture which is built up is a combination of plant shapes, foliage colours and textures as well as the more decorative eye-catching flower buds, flower-heads and seed-heads. Borders and beds, envisaged as pictorial compositions, require more than technical skills. Living plants, growing at different speeds, planted in different planes and reaching a peak of foliage or flower in different periods, need constant annual adjustment to keep the picture in balance. These schemes are works of art essentially dependent on a gardener's 'eye' as well as on technical skill in implementation; no 'blueprint' or simple diagram can reveal or dictate the complications of the seasonal reshuffling programme on which their success depends. The border, unlike a painter's finished canvas, does not present the same picture all through a season, let alone through different years. Each plant assumes many varied aspects; some grow quicker than others, altering balance

At Felbrigg Hall a border of herbs, with aromatic foliage, has been planted in the old kitchen garden.

The evolution of the border

The English border, as a design conception, is probably considered to have reached its height of perfection in Edwardian times; paintings and photographs of great gardens in this period have influenced gardening the world over, quite as much as the eighteenth-century landscape style which swept through Europe in the preceding century and which for so long has been considered the greatest English contribution to garden art. In the nineteenth and early twentieth centuries gardens again became architectural, with walls, terraces, balustrades and steps to make a frame for beds of flowering plants. At first these were mainly newly introduced annuals which were massed in garish patterns, but, by the last quarter of the nineteenth century, the charm of hardy old garden plants was recognized, and these, with the addition of many new exotics, were arranged in more tasteful colour blocks and drifts in borders where walls, hedges and lawns could be used as a background frame.

Planting became three-dimensional rather than remaining in flat patterns. The epitome of this style was the famous partnership between Edwin Lutyens and Gertrude Jekyll. He designed the garden structures of stone and brick inside which she planted cottage-garden style borders, using any available plants, choosing those which would best achieve the strongly pictorial effects she sought. She was firmly eclectic in her choice of plant material; her border designs included woody material as well as all sorts of herbaceous. Others, such as William Robinson, used only hardy plants, scorning those which needed winter protection or annual replacement. These distinctions still exist. Robinson can be thought of, *par excellence*, as a 'hardy' plant man, while Gertrude Jekyll raised border planning to an artistic level.

The most successful borders seen today, in either private or National Trust hands, have some recognizable 'colour' planning. It may not always be achieved by arrangement of bright flower colours; sometimes foliage

A view across groups of plants in the border of strong colours looks towards the clock tower at Cliveden and the paler border.

combinations, especially in all-shrub borders, have a greater and more subdued subtlety, which combined with shape and density of growth bring a more architectural quality to the results. What seems indubitable is that repetition of a limited range of colour effects rather than a great diversity of different hues turns a border into a composition rather than a collection of plants and colours. It is possible to apply the same principles which are used in overall garden design to a border scheme; linking and repetition of effects are the key to success.

Colour planning

Distinctive garden colour schemes seem to have been first thought of in the middle of the nineteenth century; new scientific theories of colour arrangement and association seemed especially appropriate for the implementation of 'bedding-out'. Massed areas of either flower or foliage (or even sands and gravel), their patterns designed on a drawing board, lent themselves to colour experimentation. Before then theories of colour and light would have been borrowed from the landscape painter; trees, sky, grass, sunlight and shadow and reflections in water had been an integral part of the eighteenth-century landscape gardener's philosophy, while consideration of detailed flower-bed colours was of minor importance. Perhaps the reasons are obvious; except for the florist's flowers, which were grown in rows or pots rather than in garden schemes, most of the flowers available until the end of the century were in muted colour tones which blended naturally together without being in need of a specific theory. It was not until the introduction of many new flowers, exotics in type and colour, from South and Central America and South Africa that attempts began not only to find a way of growing these colourful annuals in the garden but to arrange them also for colour effects. Zinnias, alonsoas, eschscholzias, verbenas, calceolarias, scarlet *Salvia splendens* and nasturtiums all had much brighter colours than traditional herbaceous plants, and pelargoniums were already being bred in vivid reds.

Colour schemes, implemented mainly in low-growing parterres, were at first often garish with strong contrasts of primary hues – blue, red and yellow – much in vogue rather than graduated harmonies of related pigments with neighbouring flowers sharing at least a hint of an adjacent rainbow hue. Colour planning was most often exemplified by ribbon beds where continuous lines of adjacent colour in concentric rows stretched into the distance or were planned in circles or other geometric shapes. These were the colour schemes mocked by William Robinson and Gertrude Jekyll in the last quarter of the century. Many years later (in 1924) Miss Jekyll recalled her attitudes: 'colour, in gardening as in painting, does not mean a garish or startling effect, such as may be provided by a bed of scarlet geranium in a setting of green turf; but

Square beds at Blickling Hall, with corners accentuated with acorn-shaped yews and flanked by island beds of roses, are planted in separate colour schemes.

it means the arrangement of colour with the deliberate intention of producing beautiful pictorial effects, whether by means of harmony or of contrast . . . sixty years ago . . . the brightest colourings that could be obtained in red, blue and yellow were put close together, often in rings like a target, and there would be meandering lines, wriggling along for no reason, of Golden Feverfew, edged with a companion wriggle of lobelia and an inner line of scarlet geranium, the only excuse being that such a ribbon border was then in fashion.'

Other colour schemes from the 1850s seem Jekyllian in their subtlety and are easily adapted from use in the parterre to taller plants in beds and borders. 'Shading – the highest style in the art of flower gardening' was invented by Lady Middleton at Shrubland in Suffolk.

At Nymans a subtle colour theme is achieved with clumps of Siberian iris repeated at regular intervals in front of a curtain of mauve-flowered wisteria.

Based on Berlin wool work, rows and groups of plants, with similar colours, were graduated through the colours of the rainbow, each separate hue blending imperceptibly with the next. Gertrude Jekyll's drifts of related 'hot' colours, her borders of blue flowers set off by grey or glaucous leaves, and her golden foliage beds relieved by shimmering pale yellow flowers, have much in common with Lady Middleton's innovation.

From her experience as a painter Miss Jekyll developed certain 'colour rules' for gardening. From Turner she learnt of the warmth of the juxtaposed reds and yellows and how to use 'blue as the colour of distance'. From Turner she also discovered the dazzling effects on neighbouring colours of the misty shimmering 'greys' he loved to use. She found that the warm bright oranges, reds and crimsons – colours situated next to each other on the rainbow – would associate most pleasingly in the garden in the same basic order of gradation. She used 'cooler' colour opposites such as blue and orange or yellow and violet in deliberate juxtaposition to make each colour seem more vivid. She liked to plant paler tinted colours and white flowers next to grey and silvery foliage plants so that the pastels appeared brighter. Sometimes she used large groupings so that colour blocks remained distinct; at others she 'wove' colours through the borders in an impressionist style, allowing results to blend in the eye when perceived from any distance.

A different approach was to make distinct and separate garden areas, in each of which colours of flowers and leaves were grouped together from one colour range. A golden-yellow planting would give a maximum contrast to an adjacent bed in grey and blue, or a green area of lawn or shady pergola would best prepare the eye for a planting scheme in complementary reds and orange which lay just out of sight. These follow-on effects are particularly applicable to garden design, where a spectator moves on a journey round the garden rather than receiving the effect of one static impression like a painter's flat canvas.

Although even in the years after the First World War – and certainly after the 1939–45 war – Miss Jekyll's borders came to be considered very labour-intensive, her basic colour tenets still hold good and have influenced modern border design. During the 1930s designers such as Percy Cane extended her themes in curving and island beds where harsh 'hot' hues 'advanced' and diminished distance, while blues, mauves and paler colours faded away

At Tatton Park different blocks of colour are separated by yew buttresses in front of a high wall.

into the landscape. More recently Mr Graham Stuart Thomas, as Gardens Adviser to the National Trust for many years, has designed new borders which bear her stamp but also express his own individuality. Mr Thomas is an artist and plantsman, and it is his border colour schemes which distinguish many Trust gardens from the run-of-the-mill and which make them so influential on modern gardening.

Many of the gardens now owned by the National Trust have borders or beds in distinct colour schemes. Lawrence Johnston designed the famous red borders at HIDCOTE, where bronze-leaved shrubs, scarlet and darker red roses, perennials and annuals with vivid scarlet and crimson flowers reach a peak between June and September. Red cannas with purple leaves, red dahlias and scarlet *Lobelia* 'Queen Victoria' are matched with purple *Prunus* and wide spreads of purple-leaved Sage (*Salvia officinalis* 'Purpurascens'). Hidcote also has a white garden, where white flowers underplanted with silver foliage are framed by topiary shapes; in other garden 'rooms' pink- and

mauve-coloured roses are underplanted with flowers of similar 'old' colours. Lawrence Johnston named one garden area for his mother: Mrs Winthrop's garden is formal with yellow and blue flowers backed by bronze foliage.

At SISSINGHURST Vita Sackville-West planned the white garden: a silver weeping pear makes a focus to a pathway flanked with scattered white flowers interleaved with grey foliage and a more formal pattern of box-edged beds in which white flowers grow through a carpet of creamy variegated leaves. At Sissinghurst further colour divisions include the Cottage Garden with the warmth of orange and red flowers and a main border in deep purple and blue. At TINTINHULL HOUSE there are blue and yellow borders, a red and yellow border, double borders of pink roses associated with pale blue flowers, and a border where silver and grey foliage, marking a formal rhythm along the edge, is a foil to pale pastel-coloured flowers.

Leaf and flower colours, used repetitively in a border, can establish a pattern which holds a design together as effectively as architectural features or architectural plants. Used in perfect symmetry these 'colour' accents will give a design formality; used seemingly in a more haphazard way these repetitions give a sense of coherence sometimes not easily identifiable. It is worth noting and analysing why border schemes work; the most successful borders will have at least two similar colour groups visible at any one time rather than a confusing number of different ones. A background hedge of dark yew or paler-leaved beech or hornbeam will unite a border design as well as being a colour foil to individual flowers and leaves. A green lawn running the length of the front of a border will have the same effect. Low-growing carpeting plants in drifts at the front edge of a border can unite a scheme; at CHARTWELL catmint alternating with *Stachys olympica* grows at the front of a border of yellow roses. At TINTINHULL mounds of grey foliage (mostly of *Artemisia* 'Powis Castle' and *Senecio* 'Sunshine') are placed in a

In the walled garden at Acorn Bank a collection of medicinal and culinary herbs are planted in the borders.

rhythm along the two main colour borders of the Pool Garden which are backed by tall yew hedges. This theme is also repeated in various other garden compartments. At THE COURTS strong clumps of *Hemerocallis* 'Citrina' placed at regular intervals along the double Temple Borders give a long season of interest with foliage and flowers as well as contributing some sense of design to a border of very mixed planting. At HIDCOTE the dark green spires of clipped yew, richly underplanted with a mixture of peonies and roses, establish a formal pattern in the Pillar Garden.

National Trust borders

The management of borders in National Trust gardens is no different to that in smaller layouts, although the size of each area being considered may be much larger. The shrubs in a mixed border may be single or in groups to suit the scale, but perennials are generally in clumps (hardly less than three of any one kind and often many more to make an effective 'splurge' of colour) which spread and need dividing every few years. In the case of herbaceous plants, which come quickly to their full maturity to give a peak performance, planning begins at least a year ahead, but small trees or shrubs will take much longer to develop their true character and quality. In beds which stretch for a hundred metres individual plants usually will be grouped in greater numbers in order to maintain distinctive foliage or flower impact; at gardens such as CLIVEDEN herbaceous perennials in the two main borders are planted in clumps of nine to fifteen, at

The sunken garden at Packwood is edged with walls over which strong-growing perennials fall and scramble giving extra height and dimension. The planting follows definite colour schemes which alter during the season.

TINTINHULL where the Pool Garden borders (25m/27yd in length and 3m/10ft wide), face each other across panels of grass and a water canal, the initial planting groups seldom exceed three to five specimens of each variety. Similarly at PACKWOOD HOUSE the flower groups in the sunken garden and wall border are small and make their distinctive impact by a repetition of key colours.

In most National Trust gardens there exists some earlier gardening pattern which inspires new or restored border layouts. Initially plans – based on an historical precedent, an inventory of plants, old photographs or the gardener's personal knowledge – are drawn to scale and used as a basis for planting groups. These serve as a guide for the first few years but need gradual adjustment as plant relationships alter. Trees, shrubs and perennials grow not only at widely differing rates but, by casting shade, influence aspects and ensure the success or failure of neighbouring plants. A Head Gardener on the spot, with help from one of the Trust's Gardens Advisers, will revise each planting scheme as necessary in order to capture as nearly as possible the original spirit of the scheme.

In private gardens of whatever size there is seldom such strict precedent or control. An individual owner working in an old garden is much more likely to change the nature of a border layout to make it less labour intensive, if possible without sacrificing interest and colour. A mixed border is difficult to manage well but easy to run at quite a low level of attainment. Strong ground-cover shrubs or perennials which flower in season are grown in drifts at ground level to prevent weed germination; over a period of years a mixed border of shrubs, perennials, bulbs, biennials and annuals can be allowed to become a labour-saving shrub border. Shrubs will grow together to prevent light reaching to lower levels and the non-woody material will deteriorate and cease to flower. Nevertheless the endless variety of shrubs with interestingly shaped and coloured leaves and flowers in season can be very effective in a scheme on their own.

The gardens belonging to the National Trust contain many fine examples in all these different styles; their comparative size and grandeur allowing ample opportunity for experiment with plant associations and plant types. These British gardens have a high standard of design and maintenance, perhaps uniformly the highest in the world under one umbrella ownership. In almost every instance planting schemes are appropriate to a site, and maintenance is almost invariably at a high standard. The scale of many of the Trust gardens is large, but, in gardening more than perhaps in any other art form, details of planting are readily adaptable to sites on a smaller scale. It is equally true that designs for one situation of soil and climate can be revised to fit a completely different set of conditions, but as each part of any planting scheme depends for its success on plant association, there is still much inspiration to be gained from the larger garden. Because of historical context many old species plants are still grown in National Trust borders, and many of the gardens have good plant selling areas where these almost 'vanished' species can be obtained. The maintenance of these gardens is possible because there is a high level of gardening interest among an increasingly numerous visiting public; it is equally true that the high standards of Trust gardening styles and techniques have influenced and continue to influence the gardening achievements of a wide cross section of British gardeners. National Trust gardens have a teaching role which is quite separate from the preservation of our garden heritage. Most Trust gardens are run by a small maintenance team – often one man will attend to as many as ten acres which will include quite intensive flower-bed areas. His problems of upkeep are no different from the average owner's: modern machinery, herbicides and fungicides, chemical and dried organic fertilizers and greenhouse techniques, when used efficiently are very effective, and can make maintenance much easier and more economical of man-hours than in Victorian and Edwardian gardens.

At Falkland Palace Percy Cane designed free-flowing borders in specific colour schemes. Some are 'mixed' island beds in the lawn, while others, as shown under high walls, are mainly for herbaceous plants.

THE HERBACEOUS BORDER

The traditional herbaceous border, the Victorian and Edwardian precursor of this style of garden decor, was composed only of non-woody plants which die down to ground level in winter; it reached its peak in high summer and, sometimes, with the addition of later-flowering perennials, biennials and annuals, had its season extended until the first frosts. In grand gardens eighty years ago less was probably expected; the important months were July and August when owners and their visitors were in the country.

Groups of each plant, arranged in blocks and drifts, were all geared for performance at this time; in the purist's garden only hardy perennials, known as 'border plants', were used, but elsewhere these were augmented by summer-flowering biennials and annuals all of which played their roles in intensifying colour effects and extending summer flowering. At one extreme the border, usually out of sight of the house and often in the walled kitchen garden, was just as seasonal as a spring garden, a June iris or peony bed, or September Michaelmas daisies; the plants were chosen for their splurge of floral colour, and leaves and habit were of lesser importance. In other instances a more prolonged performance was assured by using shrubs and bulbs as well as the truly herbaceous plants to make a mixed border. Today, especially in much-visited National Trust gardens, we would expect

At Nymans the famous double borders run down the centre of the walled garden. Annuals, planted out in blocks of twenty-five, are backed by taller more permanent perennials which give body to the whole scheme.

borders, whatever their composition might be, to give some interest from the beginning of April and to hold their colour continuously through to the first frosts.

Planning

There are all sorts of 'rules' laid down by experts which can help in deciding on a border plan. Border plants should never exceed more than half the width of the border in actual height. Staking is usually to two-thirds the ultimate height of the plant during its season of growth. The conventional modern border will still have the lowest-growing plants at the front, with careful gradation of heights towards the back, although authorities such as William Robinson, in the last quarter of the nineteenth century, encouraged a less formulated pattern. One of his suggestions was 'sometimes to let a bold plant come to the edge; and let a little carpet of a dwarf plant pass in here and there to the back, so as to give a varied instead of a monotonous surface.'

William Robinson's ideas are especially relevant when the border is viewed from two sides (as in the case of island beds) or when space is allowed for a small path at the back of the border separating it from competitive hedge roots or allowing essential access. Another dictum lays down that plants should be in clumps of uneven numbers – for instance, threes, fives, etc, depending on the scale of the whole scheme. Miss Jekyll preferred to plant in thin drifts rather than wedge-shaped blocks so that each clump had a variety of neighbours; this gives a subtle weaving effect. The likely density and spread of the

Above and Top: The herbaceous borders at Mottisfont Abbey cross the centre of the walled Rose Garden. Designed so that plants sprawl gracefully over the gravel, colour schemes are repetitive to match the formal atmosphere. They give a long seasonal display.

plant, during any given period, is usually calculated to a number per square metre. Personally I prefer denser planting than usually recommended and like tall thrusting plants in small areas. I find that when dealing with hardy perennials I look only one year ahead and plan for success in the approaching season rather than thinking far into the future. I expect to alter parts of a layout each year; others with less time for gardening will prefer a five- or six-year planning forecast. The height of plants used also depends on whether there is a background hedge or wall to give protection from wind as well as making a frame to set off the scheme. One of the most popular and effective hedging plants is the dark yew.

Choosing good-quality plants

Today herbaceous borders, especially in gardens which are regularly open to the public and in small private gardens where there is little space for separate seasonal areas, have to have the longest possible season of interest. More emphasis is placed on foliage characteristics: a good plant for the herbaceous border is chosen for its general quality rather than only for its floral contribution. Leaves and habit of growth affect the 'weight', colour and texture of what we perceive, and each plant plays a role, singly or collectively, in the scheme.

Plants from the spring garden such as euphorbias and hellebores (and even bulbs) find a place in the main border and start the season, providing not only colour but attractive leaf shapes and texture. Irises and peonies in flower in June have architectural foliage which will decorate the border both before and long after the actual flowering periods. Plants such as *Hemerocallis* or old-fashioned Goat's Rue (forms of *Galega*) which have attractive young foliage in May are at premium; those which renew their fresh leaf colour if cut down after flowering include *Alchemilla* and hardy cranesbill geraniums. Catmint not only produces new mounds of soft green after the first flush of June flowering is over but will

At Lanhydrock double herbaceous borders follow the line of the circular yew hedging which encloses this secret garden area. The mild Cornish climate allows a wider choice of perennials together with tender foliage plants which give the scheme body.

flower again later in the summer; there is even a species of Catmint, *Nepeta nervosa*, which will flower all through the summer if regularly dead-headed.

Maintenance

Quite apart from the planning for beautiful effects, perennial borders do need intensive management; plants which grow from ground level to head-height or more in one season not surprisingly need intensive feeding; they have to be staked unobtrusively and soft young stems carefully tied in. Spent flower-heads and yellowing foliage need removing. Preparation by digging and manuring is essential, and any infestation of perennial weed must be dealt with before permanent plants are put in (see Basic Methods). Heavy soils can be lightened with grit or coarse

At Upton House double herbaceous borders, separated by a wide grass path, run down towards the reflecting water in the valley. Instead of being viewed from a distance these border schemes unfold as you walk along their edge.

sand; thinner sandy textures improved with layers of organic matter. The annual loss of organic matter as plant stems are cut to ground level must be replaced with thick mulches, which not only improve texture and fertility but conserve heat in the autumn and moisture in spring.

In autumn or spring groups of plants have to be split up, divided and replanted. This can be done in sections as necessary, but every five or six years the whole border should be emptied, dug deeply, enriched with well-rotted manure and replanted. Unfortunately not all herbaceous plants need dividing with the same frequency; some such as *Iris sibirica*, *Coreopsis*, achilleas and delphiniums benefit and flower better if split at least every three years, while peonies, hostas, Japanese anemones and rodgersias perform best many years after being established. Other plants are not long-lived, or become woody with age; *Dianthus* and penstemons and most of the 'silvers' grow too much in rich border soil and slips or cuttings should be rooted each season.

In planning a border it is worth trying to put together plants needing similar soil conditions and treatment as well as looking good as neighbours. These criteria do usually overlap. Grey-leaved artemisias, silvery artichokes and thistles all require well-drained sunny positions; tall crambes, *Artemisia lactiflora*, phlox, peonies and Michaelmas daisies thrive where soil is rich and fertile. Assembling border plants is like a jigsaw puzzle, but the workload is simplified and lessened if appropriate 'companion' plants are chosen. It is also possible to choose plants which need no staking, no spraying and little dividing. As in all gardening the herbaceous border can be 'done' at different levels of excellence; some of the choicest but demanding plants can be sacrificed to save time and effort.

Seasonal borders

In larger gardens there can be individual garden areas for just one season. Plants which flower early but have strong or untidy leaves later are particularly suitable for separate

Above: Polesden Lacey's fine collection of lavenders, which are used to decorate a hedged garden area. Top: Another view of the annual borders at Nymans show the topiary crowns which decorate the central cross axis in the walled garden.

garden compartments which are only visited at one season of the year. Peonies, iris, oriental poppies, delphiniums and lupins, besides winter or spring 'gardens', are all possible. At POLESDEN LACEY, where the large walled garden is subdivided into sections, there is a peony garden, an iris garden and a lavender collection, each reaching its peak at a different time. The great summer border would have plants arranged for display only for a few months, but for that short period all the plants could flower together, thus much simplifying planning. Later Michaelmas daisies, perhaps with an edging of silvery foliage of *Stachys olympica* or *Dianthus*, as in Miss Jekyll's own garden at Munstead Wood, flower in October in another part of the garden. At UPTON HOUSE a collection of asters is being assembled for planting in a 'late' border with massive clumps of pampas grass (*Cortaderia selloana*) planted at regular intervals between the groups. At NYMANS a curving border against a yew hedge has very simple planting: bright red dahlias such as 'Bishop of Llandaff', 'Crimson Flag' and 'Breakaway' are interplanted with groups of the tall invasive *Anaphalis cinnamomea* (syn. *A. yedoensis*). At POWIS CASTLE an autumn-flowering border carries the garden into the winter.

Annual or temporary borders

Annuals, half-hardy or hardy annuals and biennials are all temporary plants. They can be a feature on their own covering the soil in massed effects inside a patterned parterre or they can be used in drifts planted between more permanent border residents; in either case they are for a specific season and as such are considered ephemeral and of much less importance than plants which contribute all the year round and mould the structure of a garden. But they have one great advantage over most other plants. This is the relatively short time they take to mature and flower, often in the case of the 'half-hardies' reaching a peak in only a few months. In spite of this, few gardens, except the largest, will give up space to a whole annual border in which soil is bare for many months of the year. It may well be very effective and floriferous, but its time span is limited. Instead most gardeners use annuals as 'infillers' in a border where, fitted round more permanent plants, they not only produce colour at dull moments but,

At Barrington Court an old Rose Garden has been recently redesigned as a white garden where cream and pale-coloured annuals such as Nicotiana langsdorfii *and* N. *'Lime Green' soften effects of pure white flowers.*

most importantly, bolster up specific colour themes while other plant groups or individual plants mature. Although many perennials will flower well in the season after division, few grown from seed can make much contribution in the following summer; they need to be grown on in a nursery area. Half-hardy annuals sown under glass in February or hardy annuals, sown the previous summer and planted out in the autumn, can play a major role within a few months. Biennials, sown in one season, mature to flower in the next. In all cases the plants are expendable after flowering is over (although in many cases some flower-heads are kept to set seed) and different schemes can be experimented with in successive years.

At Castle Drogo the wide herbaceous borders on the terraces, laid out with an Indian motif edging, are planted with perennials which have to perform all through the summer. The planting plans were done by Dillistone in the 1920s.

SUMMER BORDERS AT CASTLE DROGO

At CASTLE DROGO Lutyens designed the main bones of the formal garden to the north of the castle; a square of massive yew hedges, with smaller squares marking the corners as 'turrets', surrounds a central planting area. Two pairs of herbaceous borders lie on raised terraces overlooking a lawn in which rose-beds are laid out in a symmetrical pattern. Lutyens, engaged at this time in the early 1920s on his development of Government House in New Delhi, introduced an intricate Indian motif to shape the beds; the motif in a series of curves and straight lines outlines the terrace borders, each pair of which is separated by a gravelled pathway. The layout is by Lutyens but the detail of the flower-beds was the creation of George Dillistone, a landscape architect from Tunbridge Wells, who completed the planting in the 1920s.

The four borders, each 14m/46ft in length but varying between 2.4m/8ft and 1.8m/6ft in width, have been replanted frequently since then, but, after 1974 when Mr Anthony Drewe gave Castle Drogo to the National Trust, the spirit and detail of Dillistone's planting have been strictly adhered to. Fortunately plans for both pairs of borders exist and any adaptation consists of substitution of garden cultivars; many of the named herbaceous perennials are no longer readily available. In the early 1980s all the flower-bed soil (including the rose-beds in the lawn) was sterilized with dazomet, which also prevents replant disease especially in members of the *Rosaceae* (see Basic Methods). Every autumn, starting in September, a third of the whole border area is completely remade. All plants are removed and divided as necessary; the ground is double-dug and enriched with home-made compost before replanting. Mr Sidney Mudge, the Head Gardener (only two men work here), uses between forty and fifty tons a year for this and for a general mulch; mushroom compost is used for the rose-beds. The double borders to the north are in full sun; those to the south are

CASTLE DROGO
Herbaceous Border

→ N

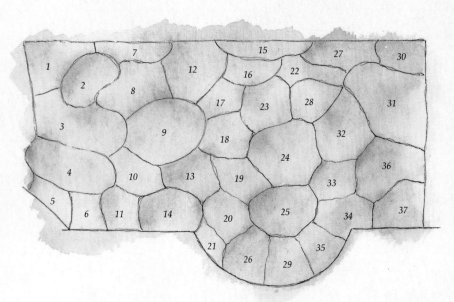

1. *Saxifraga fortunei* 'Rubrifolia'
2. White *Agapanthus*
3. *Leucanthemum maximum*
4. *Sidalcea* pink
5. *Campanula glomerata*
6. *Iris orientalis*
7. *Lithodora diffusa* 'Heavenly Blue'
8. *Echinops*
9. *Achillea ptarmica* 'The Pearl'
10. *Potentilla*
    tall red herbaceous
11. Dwarf pink Michaelmas Daisy
12. Dark blue Bearded Iris
13. *Centaurea montana*
14. *Nepeta mussinii*
15. Orange herbaceous *Potentilla*
16. *Leucanthemum maximum*
17. *Delphinium* 'Nimrod'
18. *Centaurea hypoleuca* 'John Coutts'

19. *Aster ericoides*
20. *Astrantia maxima*
21. *Armeria* pink
22. *Lychnis chalcedonica*
23. *Phlox paniculata* pink
24. *Lysimachia punctata*
25. *Geranium psilostemon*
26. *Sisyrinchium angustifolium*
27. Pale blue Bearded Iris
28. *Inula magnifica*
29. *Campanula lactiflora*
30. *Polemonium caeruleum*
31. *Crocosmia masonorum*
32. Pink/purple Michaelmas daisy
33. Blue *Agapanthus*
34. *Lychnis viscaria* 'Plena'
35. *Euphorbia griffithii* 'Fireglow'
36. *Geranium endressii*

DIMENSIONS: *7.5m × 1.8m (25ft × 6ft)*

The Indian design gives an attractive undulating effect and allow plants to be viewed from different angles.

partly shaded by a stretch of woodland which hides the garden from the long approach drive. The soil is lime-free and, situated on the edge of Dartmoor, the rainfall is high at 108cm/43in annually.

Dillistone used good hardy perennials mainly in quite small groups so that the general effect would be of colour-weaving rather than distinct blocks of colour; these small clumps make the borders very labour-intensive. The flowering season reaches a peak in July and August, although spring-flowering euphorbias and June-flowering Oriental Poppies ensure some interest earlier. At the path edge the low-growing euphorbias *Euphorbia polychroma* and *E. cyparissias*, hardy cranesbill geraniums, *Stachys byzantina*, Catmint, heucheras and erigerons fall across the gravel, blurring the crisp outline of the design. On the inner side above the lawn and rose-beds, sprawling over the terrace wall in full sun, *Campanula carpatica*, dianthus, armerias, artemisias and cerastiums thrive in the well-drained soil. Perennials of medium height occupy the centre of the borders running as a spine between the lower ribs of planting. Delphiniums, phlox, Michaelmas daisies, verbascums and inulas are given support with beech twigs placed in position in May. Taller plants need firmer staking with wooden posts and twine; these are backed against the outer hedges. *Macleaya*, hollyhocks, aconitums, filipendulas, thalictrums and more delphiniums are colourful against the green yew.

The narrow borders below the retaining walls of the terrace (see plan) were recently revised by the National Trust; a mixture of low-growing perennials grow between groups of small shrub roses such as 'The Fairy' and 'Little White Pet', both of which, with small clustered flowers, perform all summer. These borders, most visible when standing below and looking up at the main beds, link the formal square rose-beds in the grass with the free-style herbaceous borders above.

A FOLIAGE BORDER AT SIZERGH CASTLE

At SIZERGH CASTLE in Cumbria the herbaceous border, 43m/47yd long and 3m/10ft wide, is backed by a high stone wall on which wall shrubs and climbers are trained to make a curtain of foliage and flower colour to augment the scheme below. An aristocratic vine with large leaves, *Ampelopsis megalophylla*, *Actinidia kolomikta* with pink and white markings on its May foliage (the leaves become green later in the season) and a summer-flowering jasmine, *Jasminum stephanense*, with a selection of roses, provide a good mixture. In this northern county, where flowering times of border perennials are usually a few weeks behind the gardens of the south-west of England, great emphasis is placed on plants with sculptural foliage which provide interest all through a season. A large-leaved rhubarb, *Rheum palmatum* 'Atrosanguineum', has vivid almost translucent young foliage in May, with tall flower-spikes of glowing deeper crimson in early summer. At the back of the bed groups of feathery foliage of *Cimicifuga*, *Sanguisorba* and *Aruncus dioicus* contrast with the more solid green of cut-leaved *Ligularia przewalskii*, *Verbascum vernale*, the glaucous colouring of *Thalictrum flavum glaucum* (syn. *T. speciosissimum*) and *Lysimachia ephemerum* and the subtle purple-leaved form of *Clematis recta*. Kniphofias with grass-like leaves are decorative farther forward in the border: *Kniphofia* 'Tubergeniana' has parchment-yellow flower-spikes in midsummer, K. 'Wrexham Buttercup' is taller, reaching 1.2m/4ft, and has pure yellow pokers in summer, while K. 'Brimstone' is brilliant yellow late in the season. Hostas and Catmint are grouped along the front of the border. Foliage is not the only consideration; June-flowering hardy geraniums and campanulas are followed at high summer by forms of *Phlox maculata*, aconitums, asters, thalictrums and Globe-Thistles (forms of *Echinops*) with spherical prickly heads, *Buphthalmum salicifolium* with yellow daisies carried on sprawling stems, and limoniums. Most of the perennial groups are repeated at regular intervals along the border giving a sense of rhythm and purpose to the design. This is a highly sophisticated border scheme where Malcolm Hutcheson, the Head Gardener, emphasises plant 'quality' above all else.

At Sizergh the rainfall is similar to that of Castle Drogo (108cm/43in), but summers will be cooler and winters more severe. A thick mulch will protect perennials.

The new border at Sizergh Castle has been designed in firm repetitive blocks in front of a high wall; good foliage plants are almost as important as flower colours.

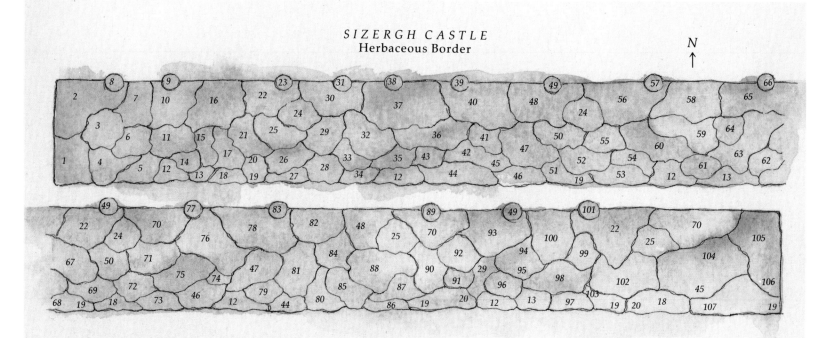

SIZERGH CASTLE
Herbaceous Border

N

1. Artemisia 'Powis Castle'
2. Rheum palmatum 'Atrosanguineum'
3. Teucrium scorodonia 'Crispum Marginatum'
4. Sedum telephium maximum 'Atropurpureum'
5. Filipendula vulgaris 'Plena'
6. Clematis recta 'Purpurea'
7. Leucanthemum maximum 'Everest' (syn. Chrysanthemum m. 'E.')
8. Actinidia kolomikta
9. Ampelopsis megalophylla
10. Cotinus coggygria 'Foliis Purpureis'
11. Lysimachia ephemerum
12. Nepeta
13. Hosta lancifolia
14. Hemerocallis 'Marion Vaughn'
15. Delphinium 'King Arthur'
16. Cimicifuga racemosa
17. Aster 'early blue'
18. Oenothera missouriensis
19. Viola cornuta
20. Limonium latifolium
21. × Solidaster luteus
22. Echinops sphaerocephalus
23. Rose 'Schoolgirl'
24. Aruncus dioicus (syn. A. sylvester)
25. Kniphofia 'Wrexham Buttercup'
26. Phlox maculata 'Alpha'

27. Epilobium glabellum
28. Sedum spectabile
29. Aster × frikartii 'Mönch'
30. Thalictrum flavum glaucum
31. Rose 'Leverkusen'
32. Anemone × hybrida 'Bressingham Glow'
33. Nepeta govaniana
34. Campanula poscharskyana 'Stella'
35. Paeonia
36. Phlox paniculata 'Septemberschnee'
37. Aconitum carmichaelii 'Barker's Variety'
38. Rose 'Blush Noisette'
39. Ceanothus
40. Polygonum amplexicaule 'Atrosanguineum'
41. Crocosmia masonorum
42. Campanula latiloba 'Highcliffe'
43. Hemerocallis 'Dawn Play'
44. Helleborus × sternii
45. Galtonia candicans
46. Buphthalmum salicifolium
47. Geranium pratense 'Plenum Violaceum'
48. Echinops ritro
49. Rose 'Alchemist'
50. Kniphofia (own stock)
51. Alyssum saxatile
52. Viola cornuta (dark blue)
53. Rudbeckia fulgida 'Goldsturm'

54. Iris pumila
55. Potentilla recta warrenii
56. Helenium 'The Bishop'
57. Thalictrum flavum glaucum
58. Jasminum × stephanense
59. Ligularia przewalskii
60. Euphorbia palustris
61. Geranium psilostemon
62. Hemerocallis 'Apricotta' (own stock)
63. Lobelia cardinalis
64. Salvia × superba 'Superba'
65. Delphinium 'Black Knight'
66. Helenium 'Moerheim Beauty'
67. Rose 'American Pillar'
68. Achillea filipendulina 'Gold Plate'
69. Lathyrus vernus
70. Thalictrum flavum glaucum
71. Rudbeckia fulgida deamii
72. Ranunculus acris 'Flore Pleno'
73. Potentilla 'William Rollison'
74. Crocosmia
75. Euphorbia polychroma
76. Ligularia dentata 'Desdemona'
77. Rose 'Golden Rambler'
78. Verbascum 'Vernale'
79. Hemerocallis 'Colonial Dame' (own stock)
80. Geranium wallichianum 'Buxton's Variety'

81. Phlox maculata 'Omega'
82. Sidalcea 'Sussex Beauty'
83. Rose 'New Dawn'
84. Sanguisorba obtusa
85. Polemonium foliosissimum
86. Geranium renardii
87. Achillea ptarmica double
88. Kniphofia 'Shining Sceptre'
89. Rose 'François Juranville'
90. Eryngium tripartitum
91. Eremurus stenophyllus stenophyllus
92. Phlox 'Fujiyama'
93. Lavatera thuringiaca 'Rosea'
94. Perovskia 'Blue Spire'
95. Pulmonaria 'Mrs Moon'
96. Hemerocallis 'White Coral'
97. Polygonum affine 'Superbum'
98. Centaurea hypoleuca 'John Coutts'
99. Delphinium 'Guinevere' (light blue)
100. Campanula lactiflora 'Prichard's Variety'
101. Rose 'Dream Girl'
102. Kniphofia 'Brimstone'
103. Liriope muscari
104. Campanula persicifolia
105. Anaphalis triplinervis
106. Verbena bonariensis
107. Sedum 'Autumn Joy'

DIMENSIONS: 41m × 3m (140ft × 10ft)

CLOSE PLANTING AT PACKWOOD HOUSE

At PACKWOOD HOUSE, famous for yew topiary, there are also some fine borders which are readily adapted to gardens of a more modest scale. A sunken garden with raised beds of mainly hardy perennials augmented with annuals and tender pelargoniums and a colourful wall border show how close-packed planting of many different varieties, in very small groups, can ensure the good colour effects for many months. The Head Gardener, Mr John Ellis, plants in threes, or even uses a single plant of something like Catmint: the large species *Nepeta gigantea* can stand alone. In the border raised by four courses of brick making a supporting wall, phlox, Golden Rod, grassy-leaved *Crocosmia*, heleniums and *Coreopsis verticillata* are interplanted with drifts of dahlias and pelargoniums. Grey-leaved alyssum, a smaller Catmint and lavender bushes at the entrance fall over the brick and are planted at regular intervals to hold the design together. At the back tripods provide a frame for some of the old forms of Sweet Pea including 'Primadonna' and 'Painted Lady', which are heavy with fragrance. Delphiniums at the back

On the upper terrace at Packwood the perennial borders, with colour groups repeated at regular intervals, are backed by architectural yews.

are staked in spring, but many of the other plants grow sturdily and the close planting obviates the necessity for meticulous supporting twigs or bamboos.

In the wall border taller plants, such as the unusual creamy-yellow *Salvia glutinosa* with coarse hairy leaves, and various yellow daisy-flowered plants keep colour going until late in the summer. Different garden forms of tall *Aconitum napellus* complement the bright yellows with their dark purple hooded flowers, while paler mistier blues are at the front. Mr Ellis says there is no particular colour scheme, but by August yellows and blues predominate with splashes of scarlet pelargoniums drawing the eye. Many of the plants are propagated from the originals used by Mr G. Baron Ash, who gave Packwood to the National Trust in 1941. It was he who created the sunken garden and central lily pond to add colour to a garden consisting primarily of architectural yew and box.

At Packwood, borders in the sunken garden are very tightly planted with small groups of each variety.

TWIN COLOUR SCHEMES AT BLICKLING HALL

Old photographs and paintings of BLICKLING HALL show a large number of beds and elaborate planting occupying most of the flat lawn surface to the east of the house. Interestingly, the parterre beds – designed by Constance, Lady Lothian in 1872 – were filled with hardy plants rather than the tender 'bedding' plants favoured in most grand gardens in the Victorian era. In the 1930s many of the smaller beds were swept away, and Mrs Norah Lindsay, a well-known amateur designer, prepared plans for planting the four large square beds that we see today. The planting in the squares is of herbaceous plants only, carefully graded for size and colour, and each is flanked by four island beds of roses edged with Catmint, with acorn-shaped topiary yew specimens marking the outer corners.

Although some of the roses are original Floribundas dating from 1924, the Trust has not thought it necessary to continue to use only plants that would have been available to Mrs Lindsay. New garden cultivars which prove healthy and flower for long periods are chosen in preference to older varieties which need more maintenance. Basically, the colour schemes are as she planned them.

Many of the hardy perennials are the same as those used at MOUNT STEWART (see Chapter 3), though the East Anglian climate at Blickling is harsh compared with that of Northern Ireland, and the low rainfall (only 63.5cm/25in) means that a moisture-retaining mulch of well-rotted farmyard manure is essential.

Mr Charles Simmons, the Head Gardener at Blickling, writes about the planting and upkeep of these beds:

'In the two beds nearest the house the flower colours are a blend of blue, mauve, pink and white, with a touch of scarlet from the rose 'Kirsten Poulsen'. In the two beds beyond, the colour scheme is yellow and orange. Certain plants such as grey-leaved *Stachys olympica* are used as edging in all four beds; a single specimen of *Yucca filamentosa* stands at each corner, effectively linking the two schemes and ensuring that they seem part of an integral design. Groups of the double white-flowered *Campanula trachelium* 'Alba Plena' are also repeated in all the beds. The planting schemes and colour associations for each pair of beds is similar but not identical. For instance clumps of *Eupatorium purpureum*, *Cicerbita plumieri* and pink-flowered *Lavatera* take central positions in both of the beds to the west and nearest to the house. *Aconitum napellus* is in the middle foreground and *Erigeron* 'Quakeress' is at the edge of both the beds. In the yellow and orange beds to the east *Rudbeckia maxima* and Golden Rod (an old form of *Solidago* – unidentified) dominate both beds in late summer, occupying the central position, but other plants are repeated in more random fashion. Norah Lindsay understood how colours will appear to change when used in different associations and she never hesitated to use an identical plant with different neighbours to produce her desired effects.

In the beds grading of heights was carefully thought out. The immediate impression is that the soil towards the centre has been raised by 60-90cm/2-3ft. In actual fact the difference in soil level is no more than about 23cm/9in. In the beds nearest the house height in the centre is obtained by using plants such as *Lavatera thuringiaca* 'Rosea' (formerly known as *L. olbia* 'Rosea'), the blue-flowered Globe-Thistle (*Echinops ritro*), *Campanula lactiflora* and delphiniums. Sloping away from the centre and providing intermediate height are various veronicas, *Lythrum salicaria* 'Robert', *Astrantia major* and *Salvia* 'Superba'. Towards the extreme outside edge are groups of *Geranium endressii*, mauve-flowered *Stachys macrantha* and silvery-leaved *Anaphalis margaritacea*. In the two beds farthest from the house rudbeckias and tall *Macleaya* are flanked with lower-growing cream-flowered *Artemisia lactiflora* and *Ligularia dentata*. At the edge the forms of the shorter *Rudbeckia fulgida* stand in front of the lemon-flowered *Anthemis tinctoria* 'E. C. Buxton'. These are only a few examples: by careful choice of plants which flower successively through the summer, the overall picture conveys the defined colour scheme from June to early autumn.

Bordering the west beds are pink and crimson Polyantha roses, their colours blending with massed flowers in neighbouring beds. Catmint (*Nepeta mussinii*) contributes soft grey leaves and mauvish-blue flowers most of the season, cutting back in midsummer to prevent it swamping the rose bushes and ensuring repeated, almost continuous, flowering. In 1985 severe winter frosts killed many Catmint plants, and these had to be replaced in the spring. The farther beds are bordered with Polyantha roses, red 'Locarno' and

The planting design in the square beds in the lawn at Blickling Hall were originally done by Mrs Norah Lindsay in the 1930s. Today her plants and colour schemes are maintained; identical or similar plants have been reinstated.

BLICKLING
Mixed Border

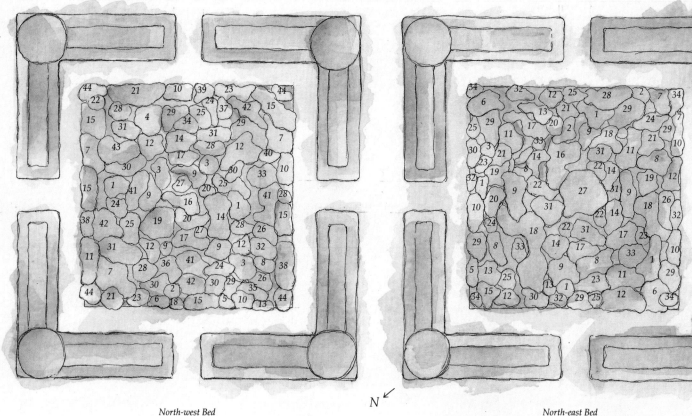

North-west Bed

North-east Bed

N

North-west Bed

1. *Aconitum × bicolor*
2. *A. 'Bressingham Spire'*
3. *A. napellus carneum*
4. *A. 'Spark's Variety'*
5. *A. vulparia*
6. *Anaphalis margaritacea*
7. *Astrantia major*
8. *A. maxima*
9. *Campanula lactiflora*
10. *C. persicifolia 'Telham Beauty'*
11. *C. trachelium 'Alba Plena'*
12. *Delphinium*
13. *Dictamnus albus purpureus*
14. *Echinops ritro*
15. *Erigeron 'Quakeress'*
16. *Eupatorium purpureum*
17. *Galega officinalis*
18. *Geranium endressii*
19. *Cicerbita plumieri*
20. *Lavatera cultivata*
21. *Leucanthemum maximum 'Phyllis Smith'*
22. *Liatris spicata*

23. *Limonium latifolium*
24. *Lychnis chalcedonica*
25. *Lythrum salicaria 'Brightness'*
26. *L.s. 'Robert'*
27. *Macleaya cordata*
28. *Monarda 'Cambridge Scarlet'*
29. *Phalaris arundinacea 'Picta'*
30. *Phlox paniculata 'Elizabeth Campbell'*
31. *Polygonum amplexicaule 'Atrosanguineum'*
32. *P. bistorta 'Superbum'*
33. *Salvia × superba 'Superba'*
34. *Sanguisorba sp.*
35. *Sidalcea 'Croftway Red'*
36. *S. 'Croftway Red'*
37. *S. (own)*
38. *Stachys olympica*
39. *S. macrantha*
40. *Thalictrum delavayi*
41. *Veronica spicata*
42. *V. virginica alba*
43. *V.v. japonica*
44. *Yucca filamentosa*

North-east Bed

1. *Achillea 'Coronation Gold'*
2. *A. 'Moonshine'*
3. *A. ptarmica*
4. *Aconitum napellus*
5. *Anaphalis margaritacea*
6. *Anthemis 'E.C. Buxton'*
7. *A. 'Grallach Gold'*
8. *Crocosmia paniculata*
9. *Artemisia lactiflora*
10. *Campanula trachelium 'Alba Plena'*
11. *Centaurea macrocephala*
12. *Erigeron 'Quakeress'*
13. *Helenium pumilum*
14. *H. 'Riverton Gem'*
15. *H. 'The Bishop'*
16. *Heliopsis scabra 'Bladhams'*
17. *H.s. 'Incomparabilis'*

18. *H.s. 'Zinniiflora'*
19. *Ligularia dentata*
20. *Lilium × testaceum*
21. *Lychnis chalcedonica*
22. *Macleaya cordata*
23. *Phalaris arundinacea 'Picta'*
24. *Potentilla nepalensis 'Master Floris*
25. *Rudbeckia fulgida deamii*
26. *R. nitida 'Goldquelle'*
27. *R. maxima*
28. *Sisyrinchium striatum*
29. *Solidago 'Goldenmosa'*
30. *S. 'Lemore'*
31. *Solidago*
32. *Stachys olympica*
33. *Verbascum chaixii*
34. *Yucca filamentosa*

DIMENSIONS: *10m × 10m (33ft × 33ft) Excluding corner borders*

orange 'Gloria Mundi', there is also a similar planting of Catmint.

Maintenance of these four colourful beds and the long border near by follows a similar annual pattern and is a procedure which works well. All plants are cut down in November to within 12–15cm/5–6in of ground level, and the beds are raked clean. Because of the density of plants there is no serious weed problem in the summer, although weeds do germinate at the outer edge, where there is light and space. Digging is always done in the autumn but again can only be done when plants have to be divided or moved, as there is no space even for forking over. Farmyard manure is spread thickly over the surface of the soil as space permits. Some plants are split and replanted in the late autumn but, in this relatively cold climate, it is safer to leave division of many until the following spring. This also allows an assessment of winter losses.

Staking the taller plants is carried out through May and June, as the plants grow, and at Blickling traditional pea-sticks are still used in preference to more modern methods. They are effective and unobtrusive. Another old practice still adopted here is the use of white painted wooden labels. These may last only two seasons, but they seem in keeping with the atmosphere of the garden and are much appreciated by the many visitors.'

THE TERRACE BORDERS AT POWIS CASTLE

At POWIS CASTLE the borders on the steep terraces below the castle wall are mixed in content; wall shrubs and climbers protected by the high walls give background colour to the mainly summer-flowering non-woody plants which grow lush in the rich and well-mulched beds. Many of the wide bulky shrubs and shrub roses, actually planted towards the front or middle of the beds, seem designed to separate definite stretches of 'theme' planting; the shrubs themselves flower in the earlier part of the season. These herbaceous areas are the ones featured and discussed; for this reason they are included in this chapter rather than regarded as a mixed border, as is the 'annual' or 'tropical' border discussed in Chapter 3.

Most of these terrace borders are designed for specific colour and seasonal effect which last from June until the end of October. This area of Wales is mainly visited during the summer holiday season: probably two-thirds of the 80,000 visitors come in July and August. The soil on the terraces is alkaline, although elsewhere in the woodland the pH reading is much lower and allows acid-loving trees and shrubs to make a fine display. In spite of the drainage on the terraces, border conditions are mainly moist and rich; conditions which enable herbaceous plants to make a great deal of growth in their short season. That, combined with rather cool nights, give a climatic aspect not unlike that found in some Scottish east-coast gardens. Wall protection and sharp frost drainage dropping down the steep slopes make it possible to grow and out-winter many plants which would prove tender elsewhere. As an example for many years it has been policy to leave the tubers of dahlias in the ground where they thrive, covered with a thick mulch of compost and leaf-mould. This is impossible in a garden such as Hidcote, where severe frosts are trapped along border areas under the yew hedges.

Mr Jimmy Hancock, the Head Gardener, finds that

many of the best perennials perform well if very frequently divided. In the rich soil plants quickly establish to grow almost too tall, requiring very sturdy staking. Many, among them silver-leaved *Anaphalis*, *Sedum* 'Autumn Joy' and *S. spectabile*, benefit from being split annually, but galegas (he grows both the early-flowering *Galega orientalis* and ordinary Goat's Rue, *G. officinalis*), chelones, aconitums, lythrums and cimicifugas are left to mature and reach a peak over a few years. Through frequent mulching the soil texture has been so improved that even when plants are divided and replanted no digging is necessary. Powis borders are a prime example of good management. Mr Hancock is able to make compost not only from his waste herbaceous material but from the leaves raked up in the woodland garden, which contribute a more acid-based humus; the organic matter which creates the humus, so essential for solid structure, aeration and drainage as well as for providing the conditions in which growing plants can absorb nutrients, seems a key factor in the obvious health of the borders. One important point is that the compost is always sterilized with dazomet before being used at Powis.

Most of the main beds on the three terraces are lined with neat box hedges so few low-growing front-of-border plants are used. The middle terrace is broad enough to contain 3.7m/12ft wide double borders separated by a grass path – one bed under the 3m/10ft wall and an outer bed poised over an equally deep drop below. In a view from lower levels the borders above merge with the colour effects of the higher levels to give an effect of a painter's canvas on one plane – sprawling herbaceous and more shrubby plants cascading downwards to meet the plants below. All the plantings in these wide beds are designed to 'peak' in July, August and September. At the eastern end, under the giant topiary yews, flower and leaf colours are from the warmer segment of the colour spectrum; monardas, a fine purple-leaved *Dahlia* 'Laciniata Purpurea', scarlet and red lobelias (forms of *Lobelia* ×

vedrariensis, *L. syphilitica* and *L. cardinalis* × *fulgens* such as 'Queen Victoria', 'Dark Crusader', 'Tania' and 'Cherry Ripe'), *Veronica* 'Blue Spire' and *Crocosmia* 'Solfaterre'.

Farther west along the terrace colours are cooler, in paler tones. Mauves and blues of clematis, *Lythrum*, *Aconitum*, chelones, galegas and *Ceanothus* mingle with pinks and whites and gentle primrose of *Lavatera*, *Francoa sonchifolia*, *Cimicifuga* (including an elegant purple-leaved form), *Veronica virginica*, and grey-leaved achilleas and *Crocosmia* 'Citronella', both the latter with pale yellow flowers. These colours contrast with the distant views of brighter scarlet lobelias, monardas and crocosmias.

The original designs for these borders were drawn out by Mr Graham Stuart Thomas in the mid-1970s. Gradually during the intervening years, as he discovered which

On one of the Orangery terraces at Powis Castle the flowing planting, edged firmly with high clipped box, stretches towards the massive yews.

On the same terrace at Powis summer perennials are closely planted to support each other and eliminate weeds in the rich fertile soil. The Powis borders are amongst the best in Britain with strongly defined colour schemes.

areas were most suitable for a variety of plants, Mr Hancock has modified the plantings to achieve optimum results.

Today late-flowering clematis such as *Clematis × jackmanii*, *C.* 'Perle d'Azur' and many Viticella types have been established on wide 'umbrella' frames which are featured in a regular rhythm along the centre of the borders, an effective device which links the design together and gives it purpose. The borders on the other side of the central grass path above the wall echo the colour scheme of the wall border. Tall *Macleaya*, *Lactuca bourgatii*, *Nepeta sibirica*, *Echinops* and mauve and pink chelones and penstemons flourish in clumps.

Pictures show two distinct parts of the inner beds; planting in the outer bed (not shown) is complementary with similar colour drifts and heights.

AN AUTUMN-FLOWERING BORDER AT POWIS

Above: The lowest terrace at Powis is planted for autumn effects but has to look good all summer. Right: This overall view shows how important the planning stage is when terraced planting is viewed from above.

The lowest of the terrace borders, just above the apple slope, is planned for a late-summer performance. In it clumps of perennials include silver-leaved *Anaphalis triplinervis*, *Veronica* 'Blue Spire', *Kirengeshoma palmata* with fine foliage and cool yellow shuttlecock flowers, *Sedum* 'Autumn Joy', *S.* 'Ruby Glow' and *S. telephium* 'Ruprechtii' – hosts for clouds of butterflies, *Aster lateriflorus* 'Horizontalis' and *A. thompsonii*. The shrubby *Hydrangea arborescens discolor* bears its wide greenish-white flowers for many weeks. Farther along the border yellow daisy-flowered *Helianthus decapetalus* 'Capenoch Star', the tall *Dahlia* 'Admiral Rodney' – named for the admiral whose ships were constructed of Powis oak in the eighteenth century, Miss Willmott's ghost (*Eryngium giganteum*) with silvery thistle-heads, *Salvia guaranitica* of brightest blue with velvety-flowered *S. leucantha* (not hardy but easy from cuttings in late summer) and tall Toad Lilies (*Tricyrtis formosana* Stolonifera group) all flower well into late September. The farther end of this border has dark-flowered maroon hollyhocks matched with the purple-leaved tall *Atriplex hortensis* which is allowed to seed. A tall white Michaelmas daisy, *Aster albescens*, is almost woody and flowers very late. *Phygelius aequalis* has become a climber against the terrace wall where late-flowering forms and hybrids of *Clematis viticella* and *Vitis vinifera* 'Purpurea' with dull purple foliage make a background to the flowering groups.

BORDERS AND ISLAND BEDS AT FALKLAND

The gardens at the ancient royal palace of FALKLAND were redesigned in the 1950s by Percy Cane at the request of the Hereditary Keeper, Major Michael Crichton Stuart. Cane's work consists chiefly of large herbaceous borders running along the high old walls and of island beds of mixed planting. These are carefully arranged so as to afford long views in what is a rather constricted space. Borders and island beds are disposed about the perimeter leaving lavish areas of lawn unbroken except for the occasional specimen tree.

The maintenance of the herbaceous borders presents problems because of the site of the garden. Close by, to the south, hills shield the garden from sun so that in midwinter the garden may receive only two hours of sunlight. The winters are severe in this part of inland Fife and frost may lie for days, being dispelled only briefly by the sun. Mr David McCarron, the Head Gardener, says that walking on the lawn when it is frozen scorches the grass severely. Since there are no paths of any kind in this part of the garden, there is no guarantee of access to the borders until April when the days are getting longer and frost is less likely. If possible the herbaceous borders are forked over and a general fertilizer incorporated in March. Towards the end of April or the beginning of May the borders are weeded and then hoed.

At the end of May 1.8m/6ft wide skeins of black nylon netting are stretched across the borders to support the plants. This is a technique which was developed here and at Crathes. It is also used at Cliveden in Buckinghamshire but is most useful where, as in Scotland, mean temperatures are lower in the late spring and young growth is held back. Here rapid perennial growth begins in June, and clumps of plants grow together to prevent most weed germination and make access for hand-weeding less vital. At first 10cm/4in gauge netting was used, but Mr McCarron has changed to 15cm/6in gauge, as the plants

At Falkland Palace Percy Cane's island beds, where small trees, shrubs and perennials make a splendid screen in front of the wall borders, break up the lawn space and give a feeling of intimacy to all the planting.

find this less constricting and it is also cheaper. In the herbaceous borders it is supported at a height of 75cm/2ft6in by creosoted larch posts driven in at every 1.8m/6ft. The netting is stretched over the posts leaving enough 'give' for the growing plants to raise it slightly as they grow up through it. The netting is placed in a strip down the centre of the border leaving gaps at the front (where the posts are concealed by unsupported plants) and at the back. It must be said that in the East Border which is very wide – 4.5m/15ft – this leaves a rather awkward gap at the back where the tallest plants will be vulnerable to summer storms.

In the new delphinium border planted in the spring of 1988 a slightly different technique is used. The netting covers virtually the whole depth of the border thus leaving no means of concealing the 90cm/3ft high supporting posts. (Here, incidentally, the net is put in place at 30cm/1ft high and raised to the full height in two stages as the delphiniums grow.) After the netting is put into place and later on adjusted in height, the ground is hoed to removed footprints and nothing more is done during the growing season. The longer hours of daylight at this latitude extend the growing season, and herbaceous growth may continue vigorously into October. By the end of October the netting is carefully removed, and in November, when the first frosts usually occur, the remaining growth is cut back.

These borders are on quite a grand scale. The blue-and-white West Border is 3m/10ft wide and 28m/31yd long. The Long Border which faces it across the lawn is 4.5m/15ft wide and 165m/180yd long but only the central third of this is exclusively herbaceous. The delphinium border is 57m/62yd long and 2.4m/8ft wide.

The island beds follow a pattern of ornamental trees at the centre underplanted with shrubs and edged with herbaceous planting or smaller shrubs and sub-shrubs. The maintenance of these borders is straightforward. They are given a top dressing of leaf-mould every year in the spring. The problem with these beds is that as they grow larger the trees create increasingly oppressive shade and dryness, weakening the growth of the other plants. Many of the trees are Japanese flowering cherries, very decorative in flower but of no special beauty of leaf or habit – some of these have already been removed. Others, however, (for example *Acer griseum*), are more precious specimens, now in the handsome prime of life, and it makes more sense to simplify the beds to suit them.

HERBACEOUS BORDERS AT CRATHES

A view at Crathes Castle is focused on the old Portugal laurel which is firmly cut into a domed shape to give contrasting architectural emphasis.

In the north-east of Scotland, where summer days are longer and nights cooler than in the southern counties, perennials grow taller and flower later. Perhaps because the sunlight is less intense, even the paler hues seem to glow more brightly in the northern light and that, combined with the profusion of close planting, provides unforgettable impressions of rich tapestry colourings. Most of the perennial planting at CRATHES CASTLE is in the lower walled garden where borders still emphasize the original grid system of a conventional kitchen area; beds line axial paths which meet at a central point and more dense planting fills the wall beds round the perimeter of the garden to great effect.

Miss Jekyll visited Crathes and described the garden in *Some English Gardens* (published 1904) in which paintings by George Elgood portray the vivid colourings of the border plantings. Today, where in Elgood's pictures roses on simple trellis arched over a gravel path to join the box-edged borders in the central part of the kitchen garden, the main border flowering of summer perennials reaches its peak in August and September. A venerable dome-shaped Portugal Laurel (surely already planted in Miss Jekyll's day?) makes a focal point where paths meet at the lower end of the main beds. To the left a border of white flowers leads to a gate in the wall and to the right another border is filled with June-flowering plants leading the eye towards a dovecot set in the high surrounding walls. Today Elgood's gravel path is of grass, much narrower than in the early years of the century, and the wide borders on either side seem part of one pictorial scheme rather than the conventional edging to a central walk. Groups of similar plants and colours are repeated on each side, not formally as in a set rhythm, but sufficiently frequently to produce an atmosphere of calm succession. Many of the earlier-flowering hardy plants such as campanulas and *Geranium psilostemon* have blue, mauve and magenta colouring. Later in the season, by the end of August, more oranges and yellows appear to predominate with golden flat-headed achilleas and clumps of yellow daisies making strong accents.

As at FALKLAND PALACE, nylon netting is stretched between posts to give support to the growing plants. In the comparatively narrow beds at Crathes access is less important. The perennials do not come into vigorous growth until the soil warms up in early June, considerably shortening the weeding period. Flowers and foliage of tall perennials conceal other garden areas on either side; in one garden compartment earlier-flowering shrubs and shrub roses provide colour and scent in June, in another shrubs give light shade to August-flowering giant lilies (*Cardiocrinum giganteum*), astilbes and *Hemerocallis*.

JEKYLL-INSPIRED BORDERS AT CLIVEDEN

A corner of the west-facing border at Clivedon. Aruncus dioicus, *six-foot purple delphiniums, yellow-flowered verbascums and achilleas set the theme in this border of predominantly 'hot' colour.*

At CLIVEDEN Mr Graham Stuart Thomas designed two long and wide herbaceous borders which face each other across the lawn to the north of the house. There are few private gardens today which offer such opportunities of large-scale planning. Mr Thomas, influenced in his early years by Miss Jekyll as a gardener and colourist and himself an artist, designed the beds for a maximum amount of colour in July and August; spring fritillaries and a few June-flowering plants especially chosen for foliage effects which last through the rest of the summer

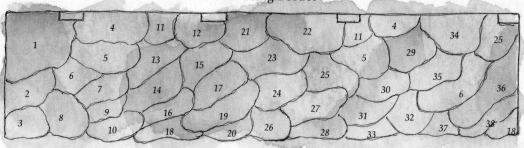

CLIVEDEN
West Facing Border

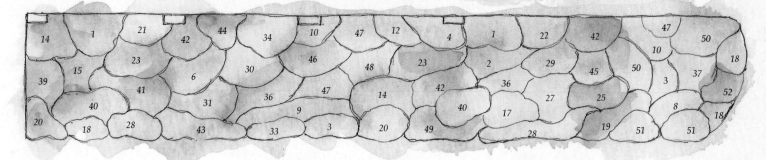

N ←

1. *Aruncus dioicus*, interplant *Fritillaria imperialis*
2. *Helenium* 'Butterpat'
3. *Euphorbia polychroma*, interplant *Lilium* 'Destiny'
4. *Verbascum* 'Vernale'
5. *Artemisia lactiflora*
6. *Phlox* four-foot scarlet with *Lilium lancifolium fortunei*
7. *Anthemis tinctoria* 'E. C. Buxton'
8. *Salvia* 'East Friesland'
9. *Crocosmia masonorum*
10. *Geranium sylvaticum* 'Mayflower'
11. *Delphinium* six-foot purple
12. *Helenium* 'Riverton Beauty'
13. *Polygonum amplexicaule* 'Firetail'
14. *Hemerocallis* 'Dorothy McDade'
15. *Lychnis chalcedonica*
16. *Rudbeckia maxima*
17. *Helenium* 'Moerheim Beauty'
18. *Bergenia cordifolia purpurea*

19. *Hemerocallis lilio-asphodelus*
20. *Sedum* 'Autumn Joy'
21. *Thalictrum flavum glaucum*
22. *Rudbeckia* 'Herbstsonne', interplant *Fritillaria imperialis*
23. *Crocosmia paniculata*
24. *Helenium* 'Wyndley'
25. *Achillea* 'Gold Plate'
26. *Euphorbia polychroma*
27. *Salvia × superba* 'Superba'
28. *Buphthalmum salicifolium*
29. *Hemerocallis* 'Stafford'
30. *Hemerocallis* 'Spanish Gold'
31. *Solidago* 'Golden Gates'
32. *Crocosmia* yellow
33. *Geranium* 'Johnson's Blue', interplant *Lilium hollandicum* orange-red
34. *Crambe cordifolia*
35. *Heliopsis* 'Summer Sun'

36. *Rudbeckia* 'Goldquelle'
37. *Rudbeckia fulgida deamii*
38. *Phlomis russeliana*
39. *Iris orientalis*
40. *Solidago* 'Goldenmosa'
41. *Phlox paniculata* 'Border Gem'
42. *Macleaya microcarpa* 'Coral Plume'
43. *Rudbeckia fulgida* 'Goldsturm'
44. *Helenium* 'Baudirektor Linne'
45. *Kniphofia* 'Royal Standard', interplant *Lilium* Maxwill
46. *Helenium* 'Golden Youth'
47. *Helenium* 'Riverton Gem'
48. *Inula magnifica*
49. *Phlox* 'Mia Ruys' with *Pulmonaria*
50. *Hemerocallis fulva*
51. *Euphorbia palustris*
52. *Platycodon grandiflorus purpureus*

DIMENSIONS: *60m × 5.5m (200ft × 18ft)*

give some early interest for visitors. Both borders have much the same dimensions as Miss Jekyll's own at Munstead Wood, the garden she made in the 1890s. Stretching north and south 60m/66yd, they are 5.5m/18ft wide and are backed by high walls where wall shrubs and climbing plants make a backdrop to flower and foliage colours of perennials in the borders. At Munstead pale flowers and grey-leaved foliage plants were placed at either end, and there was a careful build-up to stronger 'hot' colours in the centre. At Cliveden one border is of strong vibrant colours; the other has misty pale flowers. Nevertheless the 'pattern' of careful graded colour expresses much of Miss Jekyll's teaching and practice. The colour schemes are augmented by purple clematis and yellow roses behind stronger colours and by lavender-blue and pink roses on the wall backing the paler scheme.

Mr Philip Cotton, the Head Gardener, finds that the thin soil on gravel at Cliveden needs frequent mulches of manure and leaf-mould. Annual rainfall is only 64cm/25in and watering is essential in dry spells. Some plants such as monardas, delphiniums and rudbeckias do not do well in these conditions, and over the years any changes have taken this into account. In the past twigs of beech were used for supports, with stronger wooden stakes for the taller plants. More recently, having seen the successful netting system used at Crathes and Falkland, Mr Cotton is experimenting with similar methods. However, since growth begins much earlier here in the south, Mr Cotton's sections of netting are arranged to allow access for the hand weeding that remains necessary until the strong perennials are large enough to exclude weeds.

Plants such as *Sedum*, *Geranium*, *Buphthalmum* and *Bergenia* are left undisturbed for many years, while phlox, rudbeckias, some heleniums and *Crocosmia paniculata* require attention every second or third season. Other plants such as *Campanula*, verbascums, *Crambe* and day-lilies are garden thugs and need annual restraint to prevent damage to neighbours.

SUMMER-FLOWERING ANNUALS AT NYMANS

In the walled garden at NYMANS a central grass path has a border on either side in which the main planting is of groups of summer-flowering annuals which keep a good display from the end of June until October. Aligned more or less north and south, the double borders are in two sections, separated by an Italian marble fountain and topiary yew shaped into elaborate crowns. Behind the borders spring- and summer-flowering trees and shrubs growing in rough grass give interest and height through the whole season. Buddlejas and the late-flowering shrubby chestnut *Aesculus parviflora* become part of the summer scene, joining with groups of tall strong-growing perennials at the back of each border to give structure and depth. Many of the latter have architectural foliage so that even when not in flower they make a good backdrop. Among the perennials are *Echinops*, *Macleaya* and tall day-lilies. Groups of dahlias, specially chosen for colour and height, help keep the borders colourful until late autumn.

The groups of annuals are planted in blocks of 20–30 plants, all of which are grown from seed in February. The total number of seed trays exceeds 600, and these, started in heat, are then pricked out with 30 small plants to each box. Fourteen boxes of each plant are divided up between the four borders – three for each – and two are put aside in reserve. For no obvious reason annuals can 'miff' off at the pricking-out stage or later. Sometimes all plants of one variety do not thrive, at others it may only be some, and the reserve boxes make up the difference. One year all the trays of the pure-white *Lavatera* 'Mont Blanc' were failures and Mr David Masters, the Head Gardener, filled in gaps with *Salvia patens* with luminous blue flowers and *Hibiscus trionum* with wide white mallow-shaped flowers with deep black centres. Both of these plants have been a success, and, in fact, if there is time for dead-heading, continue to flower over a much longer period than the

Plants used in 1985 at Nymans include:

Ageratums: 'Spindrift', 'North Sea', 'Tall Wonder' and 'Blue Mink'
Antirrhinums: 'Kim', 'Coronette White', 'Coronette Pink',
'Coronette Bronze', 'Coronette Crimson', 'Coronette Yellow',
'Doublon', 'Leonard Sutton', 'Polar', 'Lyra',
'Tall Rocket Mixed' and 'Madame Butterfly Mixed'
Cleome hassleriana (syn. *C. spinosa*)
Convolvulus 'Dark Blue'
Godetia grandiflora 'Sybil Sherwood'
Hibiscus 'Sunny Day' Hollyhock 'Summer Carnival'
Impatiens 'White Tilt', 'Mixed Tilt'
Lavatera 'Silver Cup', 'Mont Rose', 'Mont Blanc'
Nicotiana langsdorfi and *N. alata* 'Nico Red' and 'Nico White'
Petunia 'Red Joy', 'Blue Joy', 'Sugar Daddy'
Perilla frutescens nankinensis laciniata
Rudbeckia 'Green Eyes', 'Goldilocks', 'Gloriosa Daisy Mixed' and 'Marmalade'
Tanacetum parthenium 'White Stars'
Viola 'Chantreyland', 'Giant Yellow', 'Prince Henry', 'Blue Heaven'
Zinnia 'Envy'
Groups of cannas and *Lilium × parkmannii* are also planted.

Dahlias

Cultivar	Colour	Height
'Australia Red'	dark red	1.20 m (4 ft)
'Baby Rose'	pink single	1.50 m (5 ft)
'Baby Royal'	pink single	1.20 m (4 ft)
'Baldre'	orange/pink	0.75 m (2 ft 6 in)
'Cherry Wine'	red	1.50 m (5 ft)
'Cobham G'	bright orange	1.35 m (4 ft 6 in)
'David Howard'	deep orange	1.20 m (4 ft)
'Doxy'	white	1.00 m (3 ft 4 in)
'Edith'	pink/orange	1.50 m (5 ft)
'Future'	light pink	1.05 m (3 ft 6 in)
'Gerrie Hoek'	light pink	1.50 m (5 ft)
'Klankstad Kerkrade'	yellow	1.35 m (4 ft 6 in)
'Kochelsee'	red	1.00 m (3 ft 4 in)
Large Red	red	1.80 m (6 ft)
'Margaret Appleyard'	orange	1.20 m (4 ft)
'Murillo'	pink	0.30 m (1 ft 8 in)
'Nellie Geerlings'	red	0.30 m (1 ft 8 in)
'Pink Cactus'	light pink	1.50 m (5 ft)
'Polly Peachum'	dark pink	1.35 m (4 ft 6 in)
'Rothesay Castle'	light pink	0.90 m (3 ft)
'Sneezy'	white	0.30 m (1 ft 8 in)
'Wraybury'	white	1.20 m (4 ft)
'Zonnegoud'	yellow	1.00 m (3 ft 4 in)

annual lavatera. Groups of both white and red nicotiana are planted and the larger-flowered *Nicotiana alata* (syn. *N. affinis*) 'Grandiflora' whose white flowers are tinted greenish-yellow. The early-flowering species *Nicotiana*

All the annuals at Nymans are staked when they are planted out towards the end of May. The plants are chosen for their long-flowering capabilities and also for ease of maintenance.

langsdorfii with sulphur-yellow flower-tubes has also been used to increase the range. Seed of this was obtained from Sissinghurst and, interestingly, appears to have hybridized with some neighbouring plants of *N. alata*, as the tubular-shaped blooms are wider and larger than the true species. Seed for the taller F_1 hybrid antirrhinums in single colour packets is getting harder to obtain.

Planting takes place at the end of May or even the beginning of June. Wedge-shapes are made with a trickle of sand for each group of plants and a label is placed *in situ*. No prepared plan is used, but taller plants such as antirrhinums in a single colour are usually repeated in a regular pattern down the middle of the borders, and the same colour and plant combinations are used in the facing beds. Groups of foreground plants are kept well away from the grass edge so that they will not fall over and make mowing and edge-cutting difficult. The general effect seems to be carefully thought out, yet on close examination very variable. This is because the 'key' plants establish a formal rhythm and repetition of colour groups is restful to the eye and gives a sense of satisfactory order.

Any plant which grows to more than 45cm/18in needs staking. Fortunately bundles of pea-sticks of hazel or beech are obtained through another Trust property, and forty bundles each of 2.25m/7ft6in and 1.2m/4ft twigs are necessary. The tops of the sticks are bent over tidily in traditional style. Mr Masters finds that rabbits are a real worry immediately after the plants have been put out, and the area is too large to use netting.

In late autumn the annuals are thrown away after any seed required is saved; the dahlia tubers are lifted, cleaned off and stored in a frost-free shed, and the ground is then dug over and plenty of farmyard manure dug in. An artificial compound fertilizer with an NPK ratio of 5.3:7.5:10 and containing chelated trace elements is also added. There is no winter or spring bedding in these borders, which are traditionally kept purely for their spectacular three-month summer display.

THE SHRUB BORDER

A well-thought-out shrub border can provide interest for most months of the year. Many shrubs such as witch hazel, *Corylopsis, Deutzia* and viburnums are spring-flowerers, and often these deciduous shrubs have emerging young leaves that are pale or translucent. Under their light canopies small anemones, cyclamen, scillas and chionodoxas will spread and flourish to carpet the ground completely in these early months.

In May and June shrub and bush roses enhance the colour effects and flower beside lilac, *Philadelphus* and spiraea. Late-flowerers include *Cotinus*, crinodendrons, eucryphias, hoherias, potentillas and hydrangeas; before they finish blooming fruits of *Berberis, Cotoneaster* and *Pyracantha* are already bright. Evergreen shrubs, many of which – including viburnums, rhododendrons and camellias – also flower in their own season, give firm structure and foliage in the winter months. And that is not all; many of the quickest-growing shrubs have excellent coloured foliage which can decorate a border through almost six months, with an autumn bonus of scarlet, crimson and yellow. Dogwoods, particularly forms of *Cornus alba*, aralias and evergreen *Rhamnus* and privets have golden – or cream – variegated leaves; there are golden-leaved forms of elder, *Philadelphus, Physocarpus* and *Symphoricarpos* and many other good shrubs. *Berberis, Cotinus* and *Prunus* all have purple-leaved forms and silver and grey shrubs for full sun are legion. Other shrubs have glowing coloured or peeling barks which are particularly effective during the winter months.

The time factor

There are two principal factors which determine how shrub borders are planted and how they are managed. One is the element of speed; all woody plants are slow compared to the rapid seasonal growth of herbaceous material. Secondly all the planting is permanent; each tree, bush or creeping shrub needs to be placed in its final position from the outset. An all-shrub border is looked upon as the easiest option for busy gardeners. In some respects this may be true but it certainly does not have to be dull. The idea of a Victorian shrubbery filled with gloomy evergreens separated by bare earth is out of date. Good foliage shrubs, both evergreen and deciduous, with leaves in golden, purple, silver or variegated patterns, can be as decorative as the more colourful flower-bed if carefully arranged. In a mature shrub border the plants, initially correctly placed, will have grown together so that in summer their branches meet and cast enough shade to prevent weed germination.

The only tasks are judicious pruning in summer to remove shoots after flowering and, in autumn or winter according to the shrub's needs (usually dependent on whether next year's flowers are borne on old or young wood), to keep the desirable shapes and relative sizes in the correct proportion. Unfortunately – unlike herbaceous perennials which grow from ground-level to head height in one season – most shrubs grow much more slowly. When first planted, in positions which allow for their

The narrow central pathway in the terraced garden at Castle Drogo is lined with spring-flowering and foliage shrubs which remain attractive all through the summer and then carry on to give superb autumn colour.

ultimate optimum size, there is bound to be a large area of bare earth surrounding them. To prevent germination of weed seeds, this earth must be either thickly mulched or planted with weed-suppressing, low-growing plants which will thrive but at the same time not be too vigorous and damaging to the young bush which, at this vital stage in its development, needs plenty of valuable light and air.

Maintenance

There are various forms of compromise. The strict interpretation of a shrub border obviously is a bed where only woody plants are grown; trees, shrubs of tall or medium height, and other low-growing dwarf or creeping woody plants such as junipers, heathers or spreading St John's wort (even periwinkle is botanically a shrub and not herbaceous) are planted to mature and reach their expected size in a few years. None of the plants need division or annual 'thinning' out, they are all part of the final scheme. In the interval the soil is mulched twice a year not only to prevent weed germination but also to enrich and improve the soil texture and to conserve moisture in spring and warmth in the autumn. The mulch acts as a cosmetic; it can look much more attractive than the bare soil and is doing good at the same time. As the branches of the shrubs grow closer together there will be inevitably less space for mulch, but it should still be applied as the plants will continue to gain much benefit from it.

This is one way of running a shrub border; unfortunately it is not always done perfectly and only too often contact herbicides are used as a short cut and yellowing leaves of sprayed weeds look unsightly. Another option for the shrubbery gardener is to use low-growing spreading perennials (as well as dwarf shrubs) which are vigorous enough to grow together quickly, carpeting the ground with leaves and, hopefully, some flowers in season, to suppress weeds and look attractive but not to

In this London garden, Fenton House in Hampstead, foliage shrubs with soft flower colours are used to frame steps and link separate levels of the garden.

overrun the young shrubs. These plants, much in vogue in recent years, are known as 'ground-cover' plants. Bulbs can be allowed to grow up through these spreaders. Of course this sort of gardening is not labour-free; in the first few years hand weeding between these plants is essential. However, creeping *Ajuga*, sweet, woodruff, *Waldsteinia ternata*, *Symphytum* (there are many good leaf forms of comfrey), epimediums and lamiums and many others will eventually knit tightly together and also look attractive under the spreading branches. At first, before the shrubs are well-established, they are an important part of the scheme; later they become almost invisible and, if resentful of deep shade, may deteriorate and cease to flower or thrive. Fortunately, by this time they are not necessary to the maintenance of the border.

The shrub border at Tintinhull has spots of vivid colour given by crimson 'Rosemary' rose and blue-flowered veronicas. Bronze-leaved sedums, purple Berberis *and golden* Cornus *foliage are decorative all summer.*

GOLD AND PURPLE FOLIAGE AT TINTINHULL

Most shrub borders are planted more ambitiously than those at Tatton. Low-growing flowering perennials can augment the scheme, especially when allowed to flow over the front edge; clematis and honeysuckle can clamber up through shrub branches in the main planting area.

At TINTINHULL HOUSE an inspirational border was designed by Mrs Phyllis Reiss during the 1940s. It faces east and is contained by a low box hedge and backed by tall yew. The theme is dominated by deciduous shrubs with purple and gold foliage, but groups of silver-leaved *Stachys byzantina* are planted along the front in a regular pattern. Crimson-flowered shrub roses, dark velvet-blue

T I N T I N H U L L
Shrub Border

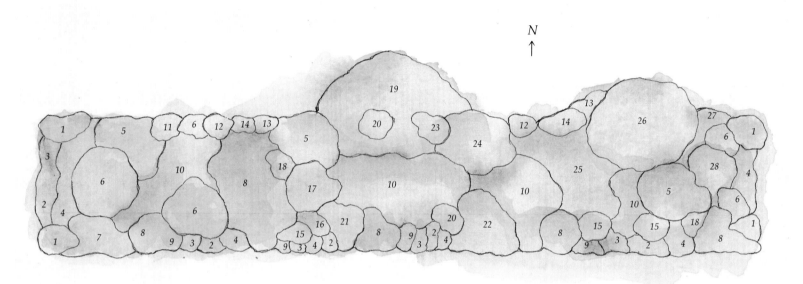

1. *Buxus sempervirens*
2. *Vinca major* 'Variegata'
3. *Lamiastrum galeobdolon* 'Variegatum'
4. *Polygonatum × hybridum*
5. *Berberis vulgaris* 'Atropurpurea'
6. *Rosa glauca* (syn. *R. rubrifolia*)
7. *Juniperus procumbens*
8. *Berberis thunbergii* 'Atropurpurea Nana'
9. *Stachys byzantina*
10. *Cornus alba* 'Spaethii'
11. *Rosa* 'Cornelia'
12. *Rosa* 'Fellenberg'
13. *Lonicera henryi*
14. *Clematis × jackmanii*
15. *Rosa* 'Rosemary Rose'
16. *Sedum telephium maximum* 'Atropurpureum'
17. *Berberis temolaica*
18. *Lythrum virgatum* 'Rose Queen'
19. *Prunus cerasifera* 'Nigra'
20. *Foeniculum vulgare purpureum*
21. *Eupatorium purpureum*
22. *Berberis dictyophylla approximata*
23. *Rosa* 'Zéphirine Drouhin'
24. *Berberis × ottawensis* 'Superba'
25. *Sambucus nigra*
26. *Prunus × blireana*
27. *Polygonatum hirtum*
28. *Viburnum sargentii* 'Onondaga'

DIMENSIONS: *25m × 4m (82ft × 13ft)*

clematis and the more azure-blue *Veronica teucrium*, a low-growing perennial which sprawls along the front over the stone edging – provide flower colour. The blue and crimson flowers and purple leaves share a common blue pigment which holds the design together. Purple-leaved *Prunus cerasifera* 'Nigra', *Berberis thunbergii atropurpurea*, *B.t.* 'Atropurpurea Nana' and *B.* × *ottawensis* 'Superba' with the golden dogwood, *Cornus alba* 'Spaethii', are arranged in a formal pattern. Grey-leaved *Berberis temolaica* and *B. dictyophylla approximata* with an almost glaucous bloom on leaf and stems, a bronze-leaved elder, *Sambucus nigra* 'Guincho Purple', and *Viburnum sargentii* 'Onondaga' have been added more recently to tone down the extreme colour contrasts. At either end large clumps of Solomon's seal (*Polygonatum* × *hybridum*) carry their white bells on arching stems in early summer. Rosemary rose and Rose 'Fellenberg' flower most of the season; *Clematis* × *jackmanii* and *Lonicera henryi* clamber up through shrubs at the centre of the border. Mrs Reiss used the rampant galeobdolon, with variegated leaves, as the main ground cover; this tends to become invasive unless tackled and reduced at least twice a year.

In spring the bed is carpeted with blue scillas and blue Apennine anemones which, in this mature garden, have increased over the years. Upkeep is a model of simplicity; most of the shrubs need pruning back severely in winter; the clematis are cut back almost to ground-level in February; the roses are pruned in late March and the dogwoods, with red stems through the winter, are 'coppiced' every few years in spring. The bed is mulched regularly with mushroom or home-made compost and farmyard manure. After flowering is over the leaves of Solomon's seal are often attacked and stripped. The cause of the damage is most often Solomon's seal sawfly (Phymatocera aterriona) effectively treated by spraying with, for example, melathion or HCH once larvae are spotted. There is very little space between the border plants so weeding is little trouble.

LOW-MAINTENANCE SHRUBS AT TATTON PARK

Mr Sam Youd manages a well-balanced shrub border at TATTON PARK. Massed shrubs with purple, grey and green foliage make maintenance economical. Curving in front of a high wall the bed is 13.7m/15yd long by 3.7m/4yd wide. A golden-leaved hop, roses and a honeysuckle clamber on the stone behind; in the bed purple-leaved *Berberis* (*B. thunbergii atropurpurea* and *B.t.* 'Rose Glow'), a *Sorbus*, *Philadelphus*, *Cornus sanguinea*, a fine *Hydrangea aspera villosa*, with foreground planting of potentilla, the rare but hardy grey-leaved *Chiliotrichum diffusum* from South America (with white daisy flowers and closely allied to the genus *Olearia*), *Caryopteris* and a large specimen of *Elaeagnus angustifolia* with glistening silver foliage have grown together to leave little space for weed infestation.

On a corner a form of *Viburnum opulus* not only bears creamy-white flowers in spring but has attractive tinted autumn foliage and glistening berries. Repeat-flowering roses are planted in groups between the other shrubs; the pink 'The Fairy' and a more solid bush rose 'Fragrant Cloud' tone harmoniously with a clump of the annual *Cleome hassleriana*. Across the lawn another shrub border in tones of gold and green is equally successful although quieter. Purple-leaved *Berberis*, *Potentilla* and viburnums link the two schemes. A variegated *Weigela* has grown large behind *Philadelphus* and pale-leaved spiraeas. Some of the spring- and summer-flowering shrubs (especially the *Philadelphus* and *Weigela*) will need their flowering branches removed in summer, but this is an opportunity to improve and control their shapes; others such as the hydrangea and roses need attention in the following spring, when the danger of hard and sustained frost are over. Hydrangeas have their flower heads removed and some bushes, with crowded stems, need thinning by cutting the old wood to the base. The branching stems of bush roses are cut back to two buds and any remaining bare soil is given a heavy mulch to improve texture.

TATTON
Shrub Border

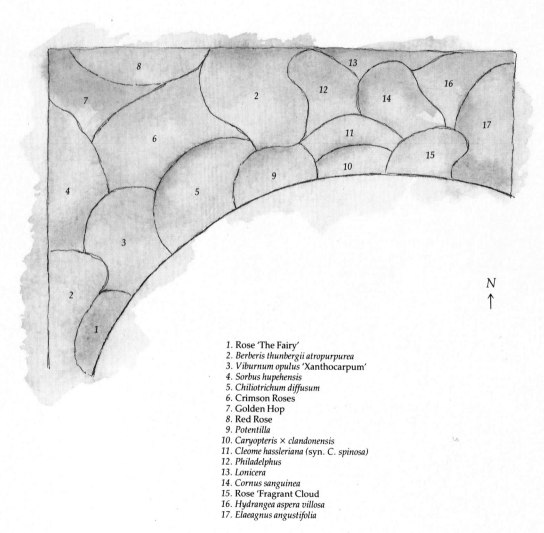

N
↑

1. Rose 'The Fairy'
2. *Berberis thunbergii atropurpurea*
3. *Viburnum opulus 'Xanthocarpum'*
4. *Sorbus hupehensis*
5. *Chiliotrichum diffusum*
6. Crimson Roses
7. Golden Hop
8. Red Rose
9. *Potentilla*
10. *Caryopteris × clandonensis*
11. *Cleome hassleriana* (syn. *C. spinosa*)
12. *Philadelphus*
13. *Lonicera*
14. *Cornus sanguinea*
15. Rose 'Fragrant Cloud'
16. *Hydrangea aspera villosa*
17. *Elaeagnus angustifolia*

DIMENSIONS: *13.5m × 3.7m (45ft × 12ft)*

GOLD AND PURPLE LEAVES WITH BLUE FLOWERS AT BUSCOT

Buscot Park's purple and golden foliaged shrubs are a foil to silver leaves, blue and yellow flowers and pale pink sedums.

New double borders at BUSCOT HOUSE, where similar colours are used, are more dramatic than those at TINTINHULL. Instead of being a single perimeter bed the Buscot borders face each other across a 2m/7ft path so that both beds unite to give an intimate visual impression which emphasizes the strength of the colour scheme.

Recently the old kitchen garden was redesigned as an extension of the ornamental garden. High walls divide the area into separate gardens and the original gravel paths still mark out a pattern, with central axes and further paths outlining perimeter beds. Covered with flowering and foliage climbers, the walls provide a background for new planting as well as providing shelter for wall shrubs. Mr Peter Coats designed the new double borders, where shrubs with golden and purple leaves, augmented by cool yellow and blue flowers, set the theme.

The plan, incorporating exactly similar 'mirror image' sections, each stretching for 25m/27yd and 11m/12yd wide, is dominated by formal repetition of tall golden-leaved false acacias (*Robinia pseudoacacia* 'Frisia'), the more rounded bush shapes of the pale gold *Philadelphus coronarius* 'Aureus' and various purple-leaved *Berberis*, including *Berberis thunbergii atropurpurea* and the smaller *B. t.* 'Rose Glow' with leaves attractively splashed with pale pink. Grey-leaved *Phlomis*, also repeated at regular intervals, with grey-leaved *Senecio* 'Sunshine', soften the effects, while a good form of *Euphorbia characias wulfenii*, with lime-yellow spikes and blue-grey leaves, provides foliage interest in winter. Yellow-flowered potentillas perform almost all the summer months and herbaceous perennials such as blue-flowered catmint, *Alchemilla mollis*, silvery *Stachys* and evergreen *Tolmiea* line the front of the beds.

Mr Michael Chapman, the Head Gardener at Buscot, writes about the planting and upkeep of these borders:

'The walk consists of four borders, 24m/79ft by 3.4m/11ft in length. The object of the planting is a mirror image. The borders run east to west. A 6m/20ft red brick wall runs along the north side and is planted with fan plums and Jefferson gage. On the south side, a trellis was built just before planting began and holds roses, honeysuckle and clematis.

The borders were hand dug approximately four weeks before planting. At time of digging, a mixture of leaf mould and mushroom compost was added to a depth of 10cm/4ins, to this bone meal was added, at approximately 57g/2oz per square yard.

Each border has a box hedge (approximately 30.5cm/1ft high), *Buxus sempervirens suffruticosa*. These are clipped if possible in April before any plants have time to become overgrown. At the time of clipping, Growmore is added (28.3g/1oz per 0.836sq m/1sq yd).

The paths are of gravel and are treated with Simazine keeping weeds to a minimum for 12 months. The gravel is known as "as dug" which has plenty of sand with it – this helps the bigger gravel bind in, and dries nearly white in colour.

The plums are sprayed with a tar oil wash after leaf fall in November. If weather holds, another spray is given after Christmas (tar oil again). Roses are sprayed for blackspot, and mildew (using copper), and aphis. Sprays are mostly applied with a Turbair sprayer which is battery driven.

Cuttings are taken in July and August and are used either for make up work or sold in a small garden centre. Most of the cuttings are put in equal parts; sand, moss peat and Perlite.

Delphiniums are staked to individual blooms and are cut back when the seedpods go brown or just before they open. *Echinops ritro* is cut to ground level in Autumn and is staked in June. All other small shrubs and herbaceous plants are cut and shaped in the Autumn. Also areas for replanting are prepared by adding moss peat and bone meal to the ground. Shrubs, if needed, are added to the borders in Autumn, other plants are added in Spring.

Wind seems to funnel down the borders and along the walls. This means that the *Robinia* 'Frisia' has to be staked. Wind burn occurs on the *Philadelphus* 'Aureus' and some *Seneco* suffers from the wind in very cold weather.

Over the last four years the trees and shrubs have grown and are now showing the effect of ground cover; this has cut the weed problem down but we still get the groundsel and a thistle or two mainly from seed blowing in over the walls. Groundsel are pulled out by hand, thistles are sprayed with glyphosate. Also the odd Wavewine is dot-treated with glyphosate or 2, 4-D with mecoprop at makers' recommended amounts.

Another view at Buscot shows the effects of distance and repetitive planting on this double border.

BUSCOT PARK
Shrub Border

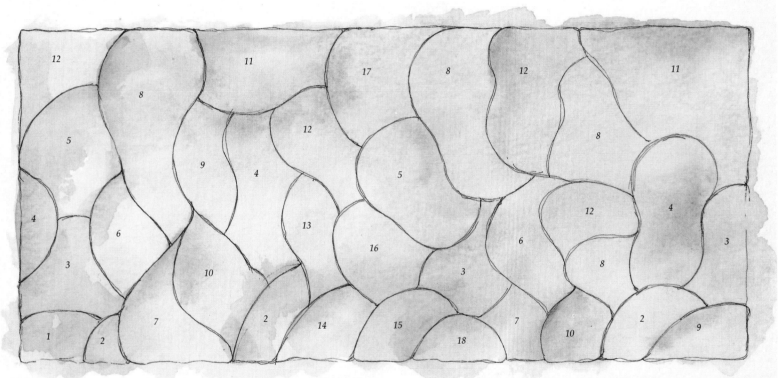

1. Golden Marjoram
2. *Nepeta* 'Six Hills Giant'
3. *Senecio* 'Sunshine'
4. *Berberis thunbergii atropurpurea*
5. *Robinia pseudoacacia* 'Frisia'
6. *Euphorbia characias wulfenii*
7. *Sedum spectabile*
8. *Philadelphus coronarius* 'Aureus'
9. Yellow *Potentilla*
10. *Alchemilla mollis*
11. *Sorbus aucuparia*
12. *Phlomis fruticosa*
13. *Echinops*
14. *Geranium × oxonianum* 'A.T. Johnson'
15. *Stachys byzantina*
16. *Rosa* 'Elizabeth of Glamis'
17. *Berberis* 'Pink Perfection'
18. *Tolmiea menziesii*

N
↑

DIMENSIONS: *25m × 3.5m (81ft × 11ft)*

LILAC-BACKED BORDERS AT FELBRIGG HALL

A line of autumn-flowering colchicums at Felbrigg Hall give an exciting performance at the end of the season.

At FELBRIGG HALL, near the coast in Norfolk, a double border runs east-west through the centre of the old walled garden. A box hedge lines the edge, and planting is of shrubs only, including a good mixture of old and modern shrub roses, except for a ribbon of autumn-flowering colchicums along the front on either side, inside the boxwood. Much of the original planting was experimental and over the years changes have been made. Lilacs make a

formal rhythm along the back of the border, although they have developed some problems.

Planned for minimum maintenance, the shrubs have grown together so that almost no bare soil is visible. Although some winter pruning is necessary (followed after a bad winter by cutting back dead shoots) and an organic mulch given occasionally to help conserve moisture (very necessary in this area of drying winds and a

FELBRIGG HALL
Shrub Border

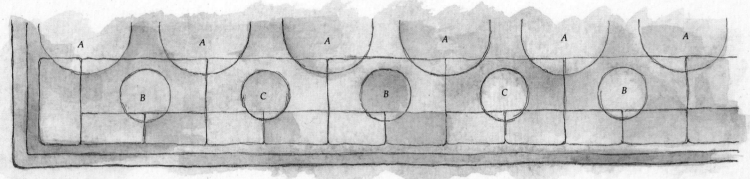

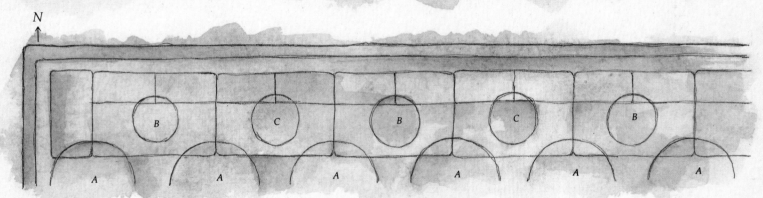

Roses B

'Nova Zembla'
'Lavender Lassie'
'Little White Pet'
'Anna Zinkeisen'
'Golden Wings'
'Bright Smiles'
'Bonn'
'Fairy Damsel'

Buddlejas C

Buddleja 'Black Knight'
B. fallowiana alba
B. davidii 'Harlequin'
B. 'Lochinch'

Shrubs A

Berberis thunbergii 'Rose Glow'
B. thunbergii atropurpurea
Caryopteris × clandonensis
Ceratostigma willmottianum
Cistus albidus
C. creticus
C. 'Silver Pink'
C. 'Sunset'
Cotinus coggygria 'Royal Purple'
Cytisus × beanii
Daphne × burkwoodii 'Somerset'
Epilobium canum (syn. *Zauschneria cana*)
Euonymus fortunei 'Silver Queen'
Fuchsia 'Chillerton Beauty'
F. magellanica 'Molinae'
F.m. 'Versicolor'
F. 'Mrs Popple'
F. 'Riccartonii'
F. 'Tom Thumb'

Halimiocistus 'Ingwersenii'
Halimium lasianthum
H. ocymoides
Hebe 'Amy'
H. 'Autumn Glory'
H. 'Great Orme'
H. 'Marjorie'
H. 'Mrs Winder'
H. 'Spender's Seedling'
H. 'Waikiki'
Helichrysum splendidum
Hydrangea serrata 'Blue Bird'
H.s. 'Preziosa'
Hypericum cyathiflorum
H. 'Hidcote'
H. kouytchense
H. × moserianum
Phlomis fruticosa
Phygelius capensis

Potentilla 'Beesii'
P. davurica veitchii
P. 'Farrer's White'
P. 'Katherine Dykes'
P. 'Manchu'
P. 'Primrose Beauty'
P. 'Tangerine'
P. 'Vilmoriniana'
Romneya coulteri
Ruta graveolens 'Jackman's Blue'
Salvia officinalis 'Purpurascens'
Senecio 'Sunshine'
S. japonica 'Anthony Waterer'
Spiraea japonica 'Goldflame'
Weigela florida 'Foliis Purpureis'
W. 'Florida Variegata'

DIMENSIONS: *90m × 3m (300ft × 10ft)*

rainfall of 61 cm/24 in), the borders are not particularly labour-intensive. The shrubs were chosen to give balanced interest through most of the summer months; some even when not in flower have good textured or coloured foliage to give interest.

Height and flower given by shrub roses in early summer is matched later by strong-growing buddlejas, which need hard pruning each February and which flower on the young wood late in the year. The original plan made in 1977 has been modified as some hebes, *Cistus*, the silvery-leaved *Dorycnium hirsutum*, *Senecio compactus* and ericas have proved unsuitable. *Cotinus coggygria* 'Royal Purple' has been substituted for purple-leaved *Prunus ×* *cistena*.

The colchicums (*Colchicum tenorii*) along the front of the border produce their fresh green leaves in early spring, and for the good of the bulbs it is essential not to remove the dying foliage until the end of July, when it comes away easily in the hand. Damage to the tip of the bulb may well prevent the stemless flowers from developing for display in September. The low box hedge partially hides the browning leaves as they die down.

Mr Ted Bullock, the Head Gardener, writes both of the routine maintenance of the border plants themselves and of the more troublesome care of the lilacs backing the borders:

'Well-rotted manure is applied only to the roses. A dressing of a balanced fertilizer is given to the other shrubs in the border in spring. The density of shrubs seems to keep most of the weed at bay so we only lightly fork over exposed areas. We don't mulch very often. Generally I keep fertilizers away from colchicums. It doesn't seem to be necessary where they are grown in relatively clean ground. If they were growing in grass, I would probably consider the application of organic fertilizers such as dried blood, hoof-and-horn or bone-meal.

The shrub roses are pruned only once a year, and up till now this has proved sufficient to keep the height and relative scales in the right proportions. I should mention that 'Little White Pet' has not been pruned for some years: we like the effective mass, now approaching 1.5m/5ft in height, at the back of the border. The same rose in the garden at the front of Felbrigg Hall is kept in check at about 75cm/2ft 6in maximum by two prunings a year, a main spring pruning and the lighter autumn cut-back, to reduce wind-rocking during the winter.

The lilacs behind the border were obtained either growing on their roots or grafted on to privet stock (*Ligustrum ovalifolium*) in order to avoid the problem of suckering shoots. Fifteen varieties were planted in December 1973. The varieties grown on the privet have not been successful due to rootstock incompatibility, which becomes apparent after a few years. Whole tops of trees gradually die back and the bush can become detached from the rootstock, especially in the high winds which prevail at Felbrigg.

It is therefore now thought advisable to avoid lilacs grafted on privet, and instead to obtain trees growing on their own roots or grafted on common lilac (*Syringa vulgaris*), carefully removing any suckers which do appear by cutting as close as possible to the main roots in summer.

Maintenance of lilacs otherwise is fairly routine. Faded flowers are removed as early as possible. In winter weak thin branches are cut out and old overgrown leggy growth can be cut back to approximately 1m/3ft from the ground, in order to rejuvenate the plant.

An occasional spray of liquid seaweed is given during the growing season, and an application of fertilizer is beneficial when the lilacs come into growth in spring. A 7-10cm/3-4in layer of leaf-mould is applied every two or three years, acting as a weed suppressor and mulch.

One spring the tips of the lilac shoots developed a nasty wilt, which appeared very worrying. Plant pathologists, however, agreed that it was due to excessive moisture, the high humidity causing *Botrytis*. By late in the summer growth and foliage looked healthy again.'

Shrub borders at Beningbrough Hall are enhanced by some strong-growing herbaceous perennials such as catmints, Stachys macrantha *and* Alchemilla mollis. *The cultivar* Buddleja *'Dartmouth' is planted at regular intervals all along both borders.*

DOUBLE SHRUB BORDERS AT BENINGBROUGH

At BENINGBROUGH HALL a pathway running north and south is flanked by a double border of shrubs (including a large number of Hybrid Musk roses), herbaceous plants and bulbs, designed to give interest from early summer to the end of September. To the east the border is backed by a wall of the old kitchen garden, and on this clematis, honeysuckle, roses and an old Teinturier grape (*Vitis*

vinifera 'Purpurea') are trained on wires attached to vine eyes to make a backdrop of foliage and flower colour throughout the summer. In the original plans the planting effects were for summer only and were based entirely on shrubs, the borders coming into flower with the first roses and with early perennials such as peonies and irises. Now drifts of tulips have been added to give a colourful display in May, growing beside emerging hosta and alchemilla leaves, and lily bulbs, Japanese anemones and *Buddleja*

'Dartmouth' prolong the season into autumn. Perennials such as hostas, *Cimicifuga cordifolia* and Japanese anemones have been chosen to contribute good foliage effects even when not in their flowering season. The sword-like leaves of yucca and iris contrast with more rounded soft shapes. Other plants more recently added include *Thalictrum aquilegifolium* with fluffy lilac pink flowers in early summer, and *T. delavayi* which bears its rich lilac creamy-centred small flowers in July and August.

Mr David Beardall, formerly Head Gardener at Beningbrough, writes about the maintenance programme for the year:

'Once the border was established the soil is enriched annually with Growmore and a thick mulch of cow manure (or any available mulching material) is added to improve the texture, keep in moisture throughout the summer and prevent weed germination. The soil, which is alkaline, is never dug; worms and bacteria do the digging. The leaves of *Prunus* 'Tai-haku' do occasionally show magnesium deficiency and the soil is treated with magnesium sulphate. Otherwise the tasks for the year consist mainly of pruning shrubs, dead-heading roses, and cutting down herbaceous foliage in autumn or early spring. The Hybrid Musk and Floribunda roses are given an additional 'shaping' when the dead-heading is done after the first flowering flush in June. This keeps them to a reasonable size, especially in relation to the scale of other plants. All the herbaceous geraniums are clipped over with shears after flowering to encourage a repeat performance later in the summer. The deciduous shrubs which flower on the new wood, such as *Buddleja* 'Dartmouth', are hard pruned in winter. When grown among other plants rather than as a specimen this particularly good cultivar with very dark purple flower-trusses and a semi-prostrate habit needs to have its lower branches removed to raise the head. The purple-leaved *Cotinus coggygria* 'Royal Purple' will benefit from spring pruning if foliage effects are required; its typical smoke-bush flowers will then be sacrificed. For maximum leaf colour and size the previous year's shoots are cut back to the lowest two buds. Those deciduous shrubs which flower on old wood, such as *Deutzia* and *Philadelphus,* have their flowering shoots removed immediately after the flowers fade. The bushes can be shaped at the same time. Penstemons flower almost continuously but need to have their dead flower-spikes regularly removed. Cuttings of these are taken every

The north corner of the main border at Beningbrough Hall continues the themes where shrub predominate but perennials give additional colour.

year in case the winter is severe.

On the wall to the east the climbing roses are pruned in early autumn and carefully tied back to horizontal wires attached to the wall by vine eyes. The large-flowered and late-flowering clematis are pruned towards the end of winter. Also on the wall *Lonicera japonica halliana*, the semi-evergreen honeysuckle with fragrant whitish-yellow flowers, benefits from cutting back in spring, long shoots sacrificed and dead wood and 'ends' removed.'

BENINGBROUGH HALL
Shrub Border

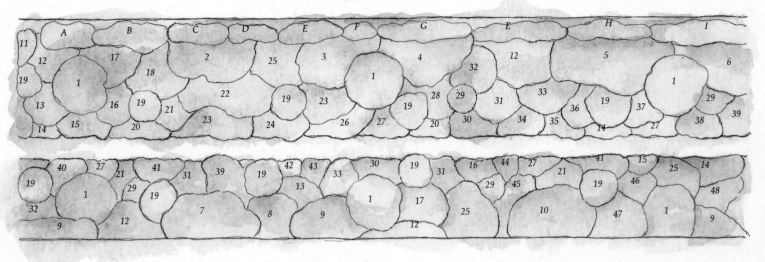

N ←

On wall

A. *Clematis* 'Perle d'Azur'
B. *Lonicera japonica halliana*
C. *Clematis* 'Etoile Rose'
D. Existing yellow rose
E. Existing pink rose
F. *Clematis × triternata* 'Rubro-marginata'
G. *Clematis* 'Venosa Violacea'
H. *Clematis* 'Comtesse de Bouchaud'
I. Rose 'Allen Chandler'

Shrubs

1. *Buddleja davidii* 'Dartmoor'
2. Rose 'Felicia' (2 plants)
3. *Cotinus coggygria* 'Royal Purple'
4. *Rosa glauca* (3)
5. Rose 'Penelope' (3)
6. *Philadelphus* 'Erectus' (2)
7. Rose 'Iceberg' (5)
8. *Berberis × ottawensis* 'Superba'
9. *Deutzia × hybrida* 'Magicien'
10. Rose 'Escapade' (5)
11. *Philadelphus* 'Belle Etoile' (2)

12. *Cimicifuga racemosa cordifolia* (3)
13. Clump of lilac *Iris germanica*
14. *Dianthus* 'Musgrave's Pink' (5)
15. *Stachys macrantha* (5)
16. *Campanula glomerata dahurica* (5)
17. *Miscanthus sinensis* 'Variegatus' (3)
18. *Geranium psilostemon* (3)
19. Peony
20. *Alchemilla mollis* (6)
21. *Anemone* 'Prinz Heinrich'
22. *Crambe cordifolia* (2)
23. *Geranium endressii* (5)
24. *Hosta fortunei hyacinthina*
25. *Thalictrum delavayi* (5)
26. Clump of purple/maroon *Iris germanica*
27. *Anaphalis triplinervis* (5)
28. *Campanula persicifolia* – blue (5)
29. *Lilium candidum* (5)
30. *Nepeta gigantea* (5)

Perennials

31. *Achillea* 'Moonshine' (6)
32. *Miscanthus sinensis* 'Gracillimus'
33. *Anemone* 'Honorine Jobert'
34. *Sisyrinchium striatum* (5)
35. *Lamium* 'White Nancy' (5)
36. Clump of yellow *Iris germanica*
37. *Lychnis coronaria* (7)
38. *Penstemon* 'Garnet' (5)
39. *Hosta sieboldiana elegans* (2)
40. *Geranium pratense* (5)
41. *Nepeta × faassenii* (5)
42. *Geranium × riversleianum* 'Russell Prichard' (6)
43. *Penstemon* 'Pink Endurance' (5)
44. *Geranium* 'Johnson's Blue' (3)
45. *Salvia × superba* 'Superba' (7)
46. Clump of lavender *Iris germanica*
47. *Thalictrum aquilegifolium album* (5)
48. *Penstemon* 'Castle Forbes' (5)

DIMENSIONS: *45m × 3m (150ft × 10ft)*
and 45m × 2.5m (150ft × 7½ft)
(only 27.5m/90ft of 45m/150ft shown here)

THE MIXED BORDER

Nowadays many gardens have the space for only one main planting area; this becomes 'the border' and is usually of 'mixed' planting. It will be planned for all-year-round interest and will include a selection of small trees and shrubs, some of which may be evergreen, as well as herbaceous plants and bulbs for seasonal flowering and foliage effects. This mixed planting, as a style, is not confined only to the smaller garden; it is found in every garden and there are innumerable ways in which it can be stage-managed. It has a much more natural look than the strictly herbaceous border where, traditionally, only plants which make quick seasonal growth from ground level each spring are used.

The mixed border can be decorative for all seasons of the year. As a design element in the garden it stands between the extremes of the formal regimented herbaceous border and the more 'natural' shrubbery. In many cases this mixed scheme is merely an extension of the conventional perennial border, and situated in an open sunny site, reflects its colourful style with the addition of a few shrubs to give permanent height and scale even in winter. Viburnums, spiraeas, deutzias and shrub and bush roses of graceful habit, with foreground planting of evergreen *Iberis sempervirens*, helianthemums and silvery artemisias, are interplanted with traditional border perennials. Bulbs such as camassias in spring, lilies in summer and galtonias later in the season complete the picture.

In one of the terraced borders at Snowshill Manor mixed planting of tall shrubs and perennials extends the seasons, with shrub shapes giving winter interest. Bush roses, pink achilleas and lime-yellow Alchemilla mollis *give a cottage garden effect.*

At the opposite extreme the border can be woodland in atmosphere, with trees casting shade to dominate totally the aspect of the site, making it essential to choose shade-loving smaller plants which spread as carpets, as an undercarpet. In between these opposites there are many other compromises both of design and management variety.

The mixed border is peculiarly 'English'; in no other country does the climate permit growing such a diversification of plant types within a few yards of one another. National Trust gardens have many examples of mixed borders; indeed most of their planting schemes are of this type rather than the rarer herbaceous layout of hardy perennials which needs, in theory, more intensive upkeep. In fact a really good mixed scheme is equally labour-intensive and calls for a high degree of management skills. If well planned, the border will have evergreen shrubs to give interest and structure through the winter months; a few of these such as Laurustinus (*Viburnum tinus*) and *Sarcococca* also flower in midwinter. Some deciduous woody plants will also bear scented flowers during this season; *Viburnum × bodnantense*, *Hamamelis*, winter honeysuckle and jasmine all flower just after Christmas. Small early-flowering bulbs are clustered under the protective canopy of their branches; aconites and crocus are followed by scillas and chionodoxas. In spring flowering trees, shrubs and bulbs are at their peak and the attractive emerging foliage of perennials, in shades of green, grey, bronze or deeper purples, adds a further visual dimension. Among these are acanthus and artichoke for hot dry borders, rodgersias, astilbes and

At Knightshayes Court a wide border in front of the Victorian house is a superb example of mixed planting where rare and tender shrubs and perennials will survive the winter.

hostas for damper and shadier situations (where soil is acid, drifts of *Meconopsis* leaves are as beautiful as their flowers later in the season).

Some of the herbaceous plants flower in June to coincide with graceful shrub and bush roses which are sufficiently vigorous to thrive in this sort of 'mixed' scheme where they are jostled by spreading herbaceous plants. Later, if they have been carefully chosen, sturdy perennials make flowering drifts between the woody plants and provide floral colour for three or four more months. Late-flowering shrubs such as buddlejas, clerodendrums, eucryphias and indigoferas are perfect for this sort of border, casting only light shade over the beds beneath them.

The energetic gardener can resort to more labour-intensive methods to prolong effects. Groups of annuals such as *Nicotiana* and *Verbena*, seasonal dahlias or tender woody plants including *Felicia*, *Sphaeralcea* and argyranthemums, which flower over a long period, are fitted in round the more permanent planting. Pots of lilies, fuchsias or hydrangeas which have been grown ahead in frames or a greenhouse can also be used to fill any available space.

Design considerations
Planning of this sort of 'mixed' border is complex; it combines an architect's sense of balance and rhythm to hold the design together through the seasons with the approach of the artist who sees the border as a series of colour pictures, for definite and successive short periods in the garden calendar. This type of bed or border can be adapted to any scale and all shapes and sizes, but management is complicated both from a 'pictorial' point of view and for the more practical and horticultural task of maintenance. There are many levels of upkeep; some borders of mixed planting can give a natural woodland appearance with very low maintenance; indeed many of these borders are found on the fringe of woodland.

At MOUNT STEWART in the outer garden curving beds are filled with massed drifts of hostas, rodgersias and astilbes and other more tender plants only suitable for the mild climate. At SHUGBOROUGH drifts of hardy geraniums undercarpet wide shrubberies and make maintenance simple (almost beyond the scope of the borders to be considered in this book). There planting is deliberately casual, each curve related to the natural contour of the slope and to the canopy of the trees and shrubs which are part of the scheme. Others, in between the 'natural' and the highly sophisticated with orchestrated colour schemes, are more cottage garden in appearance with no overall plan definable. Fruit trees in which rambling roses clamber, meadow grass and straight-edged beds with rows of gooseberry bushes beside a pathway mark a garden pattern where 'mixed' eclectic planting schemes

In the Colour Garden at Crathes purple-leaved smoke bushes are used architecturally on the corners of the beds. Red, yellow and pink flowers are arranged in formal colour blocks. The Opium poppy, Papaver somniferum *is allowed to self-seed.*

are allowed and encouraged to disguise any recognizable pattern. Today the cottage-garden style may be very sophisticated; occasionally a supreme example of mixed planting with a very natural air. Beds and borders deliberately look unplanned, curves seem unrelated and plants uncoordinated, but the rich varied planting gives a feeling of abundance sometimes lacking in a more formal and organized garden scheme.

Planting in a mixed border is in layers; overhead trees cast canopies over shrubs and the taller herbaceous plants; shrubs in their turn shade and protect lower-growing woody plants, ground-carpeting perennials and bulbs. The three-dimensional design gives scope for alternating pockets of light and shade, where sun-loving plants can grow next to those which thrive in darker, overcast conditions (where the soil is often drier because of competition from tree roots). From a management point of view this sort of planting closely resembles any woodland scheme, but whereas woodland gardens are intentionally as 'natural' in appearance as possible, the mixed border has a more precise and designed element with definite and planned relationships of scale between different planting areas. It is these precise relationships which are hard to keep adjusted as all the plant types grow at different rates. At first the quick-growing seasonal plants will dominate; then slower-growing woody plants gradually increase their spread and, casting more shade as they mature, will discourage more ephemeral neighbouring plants from flowering or even thriving.

Maintenance and adjustment

In every case an owner or gardener has to decide on the importance of keeping some control of the original plan. In some borders trees and shrubs will be allowed to grow together naturally over the years, excluding light and preventing weed germination. Some ground-cover plants with good textured and coloured leaves will thrive in the shade under their branches.

In the lower garden at Powis Castle another border with delphiniums, salvias and creamy sisyrinchiums is backed by a brick wall.

This sort of gardening is relatively labour-free; there is no necessity to dig and annual maintenance consists of mulching any remaining bare earth and judicious pruning of shrubs. Biennials are encouraged to seed and flower *in situ*; and annuals with a flexible time scale are perfect 'infillers' for border improvement.

The success of the mixed scheme depends on careful planning from the beginning, based on an understanding of how plants will change and grow each year and on their individual requirements. The really successful mixed border alters every season as the gardener shuffles and reassembles the plants which do not resent disturbance around the permanent feature-plants which gradually come to dominate the layout. As the woody plants grow it is necessary to increase the area of clumps of neighbouring bulbs and perennials in order to keep the design in balance and harmony. This means, at intervals, sacrificing some material originally part of the scheme. This sort of planting needs constant adjustment; no 'blueprint' can provide a complete programme for the years ahead and do justice to changing circumstances. The perennials and bulbs chosen can be particularly suitable; those perennials which do improve their flowering performance if divided every few years are put in beside those foliage plants which make attractive sweeps through the border; the former can have their position changed when they are divided while the rate of growth of the latter may synchronize nicely with a tree or shrub's spreading canopy. Day-lilies, astilbes, *Alchemilla*, *Brunnera macrophylla*, the invasive *Buglossoides purpurocaerulea*, hostas, *Symphytum grandiflorum*, periwinkle, *Ajuga* and even sweet-scented violets are all spreaders which keep the scale of the border scheme in balance and need little attention.

Wall borders

'Mixed' borders existed long before they were defined as a definite stylistic feature. Borders under the windows of a house or at the base of some decorative wall were usually recognized as suitable sites for climbers to make vertical curtains of foliage and flower, tender wall shrubs which needed protection, architectural shrubs to act as buttresses and anchor a house to the ground, a selection of bulbs which liked the dry soil and perennials and annuals in any remaining space. When taken over by the Trust, many large houses had beds of this sort existing alongside the bedding-out schemes in the more centrally placed parterres which were designed to be looked down on from the house.

Paintings by George Elgood at the end of the nineteenth century show borders of some of the great houses. Those at HARDWICK HALL and MONTACUTE HOUSE, today administered by the Trust, show typically 'mixed' planting. Elgood's borders in the forecourt at Hardwick Hall were described by Gertrude Jekyll in *Some English Gardens*. Backed by high walls on which climbing roses, honeysuckle and clematis twined, planting includes standard roses, *Macleaya*, mulleins and Japanese anemones, with foreground planting of pinks, tufted pansies and mignonette.

Today at Hardwick the schemes are more firmly Jekyllian in their colour scope and range. The Head Gardener, Mr Robin Allan, manages the wide borders for a lengthy seasonal display. Large shrubs such as magnolias, *Clerodendrum*, evergreen viburnums and spreading shrub roses give depth and density. Sculptural leaves of *Acanthus*, *Bergenia*, *Crambe cordifolia*, hostas and *Echinops*, planted in massive groups, match the scale of the border and very effectively anchor house and garden walls to the ground. There are still plenty of flowers from good hardy perennials, many of them already in garden use in 1900. Thalictrums, aconitums, *Macleaya*, *Aruncus dioicus* and *Artemisia lactiflora* perform in season and clematis and roses still climb on the walls. In the shade of the cedar, *Hosta sieboldiana*, with bluish almost corrugated leaves, is planted not only to fill the border, but to create the impression of rippling waves.

At Hardwick Hall the forecourt planting has been in a mixed style since 1900, when it was portrayed by George Elgood (reproduced in Some English Gardens *by Gertrude Jekyll 1904) and described by Miss Jekyll. The borders may well have had similar planting schemes since the house was built in the sixteenth century, even if the actual plants available in Elizabethan England were much more restricted and very different. Today strong growing wall shrubs buttress the walls and are underplanted with hostas (originally from Japan in the nineteenth century), cimicifuga (from both North America and Asia), dahlias from Mexico and countless other exotics which, with flower and leaf colour, produce dramatic effects. These richly planted wall-borders can be adapted for a garden of any size.*

FORECOURT BORDERS AT MONTACUTE

At Montacute, also painted for Some English Gardens *by George Elgood, where he showed a mixture of sunflowers and other ephemeral planting, the borders are today planned in more identifiable colour blocks.*

At MONTACUTE Elgood painted a bright border which edged the east forecourt where sunflowers, evening primroses (the biennial *Oenothera biennis*), border phlox and campanula, pansies and pinks were all tightly packed together. A large green shrub gives bulk and solidity but is the only visible concession to the vast scale of surrounding architecture. The forecourt borders have recently been replanted. As the ground was badly infested with bindweed and other perennial weeds, it was treated with dazomet and replanted in 1982 to a plan made originally after the 1939-45 war by Mrs Phyllis Reiss, the creator of the gardens at Tintinhull House nearby. Interested in colour association, Mrs Reiss used purplish foliage shrubs and bright flowers to tone with the golden Ham stone, excavated from the quarry above Montacute, which she felt made paler tints and grey foliage seem insipid.

The two 2.25m/7ft wide borders lie in full sun for most of the day and stretch away from the house walls. The mixed planting is very closely related in style to perennial borders; no small trees are planted and shade from spreading shrubs is not a problem. Perennials have to be firmly staked as wind funnels and turbulence sweep round corners and gateway openings. There are rain-shadows at the base of screening walls but the thick foliage of foreground shrubs and tall herbaceous plants keep these areas moist and shady. The planting scheme is dominated by purple-leaved forms of *Cotinus coggygria*, scarlet bush roses such as 'Frensham' and *Berberis thunbergii atropurpurea*; round the base of each, vigorous day-lilies (the old *Hemerocallis fulva* 'Flore Pleno'), yellow achilleas and scarlet penstemons need their clumps adjusting as the slow-growing smoke bushes and barberries mature. Groups of red dahlias are companions to the roses which are pruned severely each spring. On the walls behind and curling up the finials *Clematis* × *jackmanii*, with rich violet velvety flowers in summer, make further focal points and the large-leaved autumn-colouring vine

Vitis coignetiae, provides a curtain of October colour. Dr Mules' aubrieta (*Aubrieta deltoidea* 'Dr Mules'), irises, peonies, clumps of a fine *Erigeron*, *Erigeron* 'Dignity' with dark mauve flowers in July, are planted along the front of the border and spread over the edge of the wide gravel pathways. More flower-beds join the corner gazebos to complete the fourth side of the forecourt where there was once a seventeenth-century gatehouse. Tall yuccas – a pair of *Yucca recurvifolia* – frame a central gateway and the borders are planted in a similar style but with quieter colours to allow the eye to travel over them into the parkland beyond the garden perimeter. The brightest colour is given by groups of rose 'Orange Triumph' and clumps of pale yellow dahlia. *Erigeron* 'Sincerity', *Aster* × *frikartii* 'Mönch' and *Veronica spicata incana* with silvery leaves edge the beds; the giant seakale (*Crambe cordifolia*), tall *Macleaya* and *Acanthus spinosus* with pink spires give architectural form to the back of the borders. These thrusting perennials need continual chopping back, with fork or spade, to prevent them from damaging shrubs such as dark violet-blue *Caryopteris* × *clandonensis* 'Ferndown' and *Hypericum* 'Hidcote' with wide yellow saucers in summer.

Mr Graham Kendall, the Head Gardener keeps maintenance low although he sprays and feeds regularly. Achilleas and phlox are all given pea-sticks as supports in May; peonies and sedums have stronger metal hoops which become invisible as the foliage grows, dahlias are staked with traditional wooden sticks. With a limited gardening staff, who spend much of winter clipping yew hedges and topiary, there is no time at Montacute to mulch all the beds each season. A recent outbreak of *Verticillium* Wilt, a soil-borne disease which attacks roots, is worrying. Die-back on Smoke Bushes and *Berberis* and failure of perennials in the borders are attributed to this fungus; there is no certain cure except total replacement of the soil. At Montacute this would involve digging up the adjacent gravel paths and would be a daunting task.

MONTACUTE HOUSE
Mixed Border

Border A

Border B

N ←

N ↑

Border A

1. *Veronica spicata incana* (6)
2. *Dahlia* single yellow (3)
3. Own *Yucca*
4. *Acanthus spinosus* (6)
5. *Erigeron* 'Sincerity' (6)
6. *Alyssum saxatile citrinum* (3)
7. *Iris pallida pallida* (syn. *I.p. dalmatica*) (6)
8. *Paeonia lactiflora* white (3)
9. *Caryopteris* × *clandonensis* 'Ferndown' (4)
10. *Macleaya microcarpa* (6)
11. *Thalictrum flavum glaucum* (5)
12. *Hypericum* 'Hidcote' (3)
13. *Geum* 'Fire Opal' (5)
14. *Aubrieta* 'Dr Mules' (3)
15. *Aster* × *frikartii* 'Mönch' (6)
16. Rose 'Orange Triumph' (5)
17. *Berberis thunbergii atropurpurea*
18. *Crambe cordifolia* (3)
19. *Clematis recta* (5)

Border B

1. *Heuchera* 'Red Spangles'
2. *Caryopteris* × *clandonensis* 'Ferndown'
3. *Monarda* 'Cambridge Scarlet'
4. *Aconitum* 'Spark's Variety'
5. *Lupinus* 'Thundercloud'
6. *Fuchsia* 'Mrs Popple'
7. *Aubrieta*
8. *Euphorbia polychroma*
9. *Achillea* 'Coronation Gold'
10. Standard Honeysuckle
11. *Clematis recta*
12. *Clematis macropetala*
13. *Heliopsis* 'Gold Green Heart'
14. *Vitis vinifera* 'Purpurea'
15. *Dahlia* 'Clair de Lune'
16. *Iris pallida pallida*
17. *Geranium ibericum*
18. *Sedum* 'Autumn Joy'
19. Rose 'Frensham'
20. *Macleaya microcarpa*
21. *Lupinus* 'Gold Dust'
22. *Rudbeckia fulgida speciosa*

23. *Erigeron* 'Dignity'
24. *Hemerocallis* 'Flore Pleno'
25. *Cotinus coggygria* 'Royal Purple'
26. *Clematis* × *jackmanii*
27. *Vitis* 'Brant'
28. *Acanthus spinosus*
29. *Phlox paniculata* 'San Antonio'
30. *Veronica spicata*
31. *Erysimum* 'Moonlight'
32. *Dahlia* 'John Street'
33. *Delphinium* 'Molly Buchanan'
34. *Salvia* × *superba*
35. *Paeonia* white
36. *Thalictrum flavum glaucum*
37. *Phlox paniculata* 'Starfire'
38. *Coreopsis verticillata*
39. *Penstemon* 'Garnet'
40. *Berberis thunbergii atropurpurea*
41. *Delphinium* 'Nimrod'
42. *Thalictrum delavayi*
43. Existing *Paeonia delavayi lutea*

DIMENSIONS: 142m × 2.35m (464ft × 7½ft) *Entire Border*

THE ORCHARD BORDER AT ACORN BANK

Above: The walled garden at Acorn Bank is treated as an informal orchard area where wall shrubs, perennials and bulbs have a deliberately rustic and unsophisticated atmosphere. Right: The same effects are achieved in the walled Herb Garden where, although decorative with attractive and aromatic foliage plants much in evidence, planning is primarily for 'useful' plants.

At ACORN BANK in Cumbria the border style, with very similar shrubs, roses and perennials, has a more domestic atmosphere in keeping with the humbler rose-grey sandstone house. Rainfall at Acorn Bank is high at 108cm/43in (at Montacute it is only 73cm/29in) and cold winds sweep through the surrounding fell country. The sheltered walled garden to the east of the house dates from the seventeenth century and in it grow old forms of apples such as the local 'Keswick Codling', 'Norfolk Beefing' and the rare 'Scotch Bridget', with Jargonelle pears (*Pyrus communis* 'Jargonelle') and greengages, medlars, Portugal and Vranja quinces and mulberries. A central avenue of a double white cherry, *Prunus cerasus* 'Rhexii', known since

the sixteenth century, lines the centre of the garden and divides the orchard in two. The native tulip, *Tulipa sylvestris*, wood anemone (*Anemone nemorosa* and its double form *A.n.* 'Vestal') and Pheasant Eye *Narcissus* have naturalized in the grass in the alkaline clay soil. The borders lie under the main perimeter walls where old espalier fruit still survive to give architectural interest.

Recent planting of climbing and rambling roses and clematis make a backdrop to the border plants. Bushes of *Philadelphus*, lilacs, weigelas, spiraeas, *Berberis* and Hybrid Musk roses with a few purple-leaved *Cotinus* give a pleasant gentle effect very different from the more forceful colour sequences at Montacute. The flower colouring throughout has a period flavour – magentas, mauves and pinks avoiding all the more strident modern tones and suiting the orchard flavour of the garden. Between the shrubs *Thalictrum delavayi* 'Hewitt's Double', *Geranium psilostemon* and *Veratrum nigrum* are planted in full sun, while hostas, Japanese anemones, *Kirengeshoma palmata* and astilbes face north-west in a cooler site.

The herb garden at ACORN BANK was begun in the 1960s, but mainly developed in the 1970s to replace a small vegetable garden. A special feature is the Trust's largest selection of herbs and medicinal plants, including a large variety of aromatic-leaved trees and shrubs as well as the usual perennial herbs. Annuals such as calendula, chervil, borage and basil are encouraged to seed freely, and height is given to the beds by quince trees and damsons.

Mr Christopher Braithwaite, the Head Gardener at Acorn Bank, writes about the conditions in which the herbs are grown:

The herb garden contains culinary and medicinal herbs grown in three different beds, separated by gravel paths. Most are woody shrubs or perennials but annuals such as calendula, chervil, borage and basil are encouraged to seed freely. Some, in fact, such as thornapple (*Datura stramonium*) and poppy resent being transplanted even as seedlings. Against the south-facing wall, in the past heated with flues to protect fruit blossom from late frosts, the bed is hot and gets baked in summer. The central bed is half-shaded but the bed along the south-west wall is in the dense shade cast by canopies of quince and damsons. Many plants used for medicinal purposes, among which are many British natives, require rich soil and good drainage rather than the full sun associated with the aromatic-leaved Mediterranean-types.

BLUE AND WHITE FLOWERS AT THE COURTS

A semi-circle of yew hedging rounds off one side of the main lawn at THE COURTS, and provides a background to a mixed planting of shrubs and perennials all chosen for their blue and white flowers. Protruding buttresses of yew further divide the curving border and make architectural 'pockets' for planting of feathery-plumed creamy *Artemisia lactiflora*, dark purple aconitums, white phlox and rounded bushes of *Caryopteris* with grey-green leaves and pale blue flowers. The bed is edged with Catmint and lavender, both of which spill forward on to the stone paving in which a central bed is massed with *Limonium latifolium*, the flowering panicles making a cloud of lavender-blue above ground-hugging green rosettes in summer. This scheme is divided from the main lawn by a bed planted with *Festuca glauca*, a tufted grass, with slender grey-green leaves.

Under the care of Mr Andrew Humphris, the new Head Gardener, this whole area of the garden, neglected and overcrowded over a period of years, has been replanted recently. All the plants (except for the yew) were removed and the invasive perennial bindweed was eradicated by spot-spraying with glyphosate. The beds were dug and farmyard manure incorporated; a further organic fertilizer was forked into the topmost layer of soil before planting. With dense planting, little bare earth remains for weed-seed germination; hoeing twice in the summer season keeps the bed in good shape. The *Caryopteris* is annually cut back severely to two buds in April, and aconitums are given support with pea-sticks in early June. Otherwise maintenance involves cutting down dead stems of herbaceous plants in autumn or spring and their division, with the clumps of grasses, every three or four years. This effective planting shows the merit of choosing a simple but immediately recognisable colour theme. A note of formality is introduced by repetition but the actual plants and their grouping remain relaxed in style.

THE COURTS
Mixed Border

1. *Lamium maculatum* 'Beacon Silver'
2. *Rosa glauca*
3. Lavender
4. *Artemisia lactiflora*
5. *Nepeta*
6. *Physostegia virginiana* 'Alba'
7. *Sedum* 'Autumn Joy'
8. *Caryopteris × clandonensis*
9. Semi-circular Yew hedge with 6 Yew buttresses
10. *Aconitum napellus*
11. *Lavandula angustifolia* 'Munstead'
12. *Aconitum carmichaelii*
13. White *Phlox paniculata*
14. *Catalpa bignonioides*
15. *Limonium latifolium*
16. *Festuca glauca*

N
↑

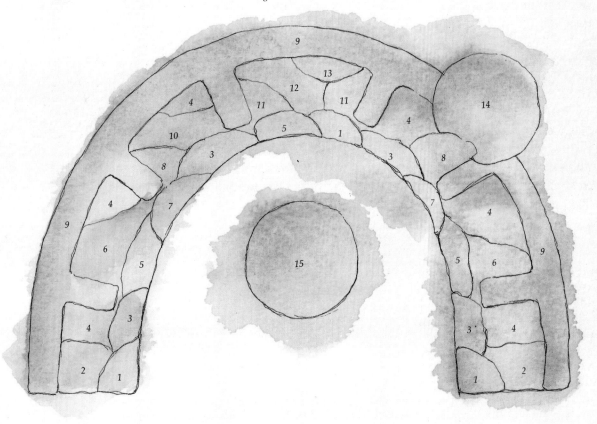

DIMENSIONS: *6m × 8.3m (19½ft × 27ft)*
Width of curved border and
diameter of central bed 2.35m (7½ft)

The red and yellow mixed border at Tintinhull House is given further colour intensity by a repetitive planting of silvery Artemisia *placed along the front edge.*

CONTRASTING COLOUR AT TINTINHULL

In the pool garden at TINTINHULL HOUSE, two equal-sized borders, both backed by tall yew hedges and edged with wide panels of grass, face each other across a rectangular canal. Designed by Mrs Phyllis Reiss after the 1939-45 war, they are planned for flower and foliage 'colour' effects. In the east-facing bed colours are predominantly 'hot' – deep yellow, orange, scarlet and crimson. In the west-facing border pastel flowers and pale leaves are in marked contrast. Primrose-yellow *Anthemis* and silver- and grey-leaved senecios and artemisias, planted in repetitive groups in both borders, give a sense of unity to the overall design of the scheme.

Tulips emerge early to flower at the beginning of May and in their colours give a hint of the colour themes which will predominate in each of the borders through the summer months. In the 'hot' east-facing bed tulip 'Queen of Night' has subtle velvety-maroon, almost black flowers. Orange summer-flowering lilies – including *Lilium lancifolium fortunei* and *L. henryi* – grow between groups of scarlet 'Frensham' roses and behind sprawling plants of *Potentilla* 'Gibson's Scarlet'. Yellow flowers, especially forms of *Compositae* with daisy flowers, are used freely, but paler lemon-yellow of *Hemerocallis citrina*, lime-yellow *Alchemilla mollis* and fluffy cream plumes of *Artemisia lactiflora* cool down the scheme. The golden variegated foliage of *Symphoricarpos orbiculatus* 'Foliis Variegatis' and golden leaves of *Sambucus racemosa* 'Plumosa Aurea' (cut hard back each winter) contribute all through the summer months. *Penstemon* 'Scarlet Fire' and the deeper red *P.* 'Garnet' may survive a mild winter, but cuttings over-wintered in a cold frame and planted out in May generally perform better than old plants. Scarlet dahlias, such as 'Grenadier' and 'Bishop of Llandaff', are planted out together with groups of the tender *Salvia fulgens* and crimson tobacco flowers after the last frost (late May is generally considered safe).

In the 'cool' border silvery-pink tulip 'Queen of Bartigons' sets the paler tone early in the season. Later galegas, thalictrums, *Campanula lactiflora*, *Achillea ptarmica* 'The Pearl', with strong clumps of mauve and of white phlox, combine with Hybrid Musk roses and tall miscanthus grass to contribute interest. By August *Aster × frikartii* 'Mönch' bears lavender-blue daisy flowers in front of tall clumps of *Eupatorium purpureum* 'Atropurpureum' with dark rich pink flowers. Groups of the pink *Dahlia* 'Gerrie Hoek' are arranged behind lower-growing plants, and pale-flowered penstemons and pink diascias fall across the stone edging at the front. Today a purple-leaved plum *Prunus cerasifera* 'Pissardii' towers from behind the yew hedge which backs this border, so darker-flowered plants such as violet *Salvia* 'superba' and the annual *Verbena rigida* become a necessary link with the heavy colour of the tree foliage.

It is unlikely that either of these beds were emptied and dug over between 1960 and 1980. During that period many of the shrubs had become large and woody and some of the more vigorous herbaceous perennials had also developed woody crowns and were flowering less profusely. There was little space for those additional 'fillers-in', the good summer-flowering annuals which prolong and extend the performance of mixed borders. It seemed essential, rather than replanting small areas at a time to tackle each border as a whole. In 1980 the 'hot' border was emptied, dug over to a depth of two spits, manured and treated with Dazomet against replant disease, being covered with polythene sheeting for part of the summer of 1981. Planting, with a new plan, based on old photographs and plant lists, began in the following autumn and was completed in the spring in time for a new season. In the same autumn the 'cool' border was treated in the same way, although now it was found possible to perform the 'cleaning' operation during September and replant the next spring. Since 1982 shrubs have remained *in situ* but many perennial clumps are frequently lifted and divided.

Across the water canal at Tintinhull the border colour scheme is more restrained with blocks of pale pastel flowers enhanced by grey and silver leaves.

RED BORDERS AT HIDCOTE

At Hidcote the famous red borders are of mixed planting, with shrubs, roses, perennials, and annuals.

There are many National Trust borders which depend on supplementary temporary planting for their greatest and most long-lasting summer effects. At HIDCOTE MANOR much of the seasonal colour in the Red Borders, reaching a peak in August, comes from temporary planting. *Prunus* with purple leaves (*Prunus spinosa* 'Purpurea'), purple forms of *Cotinus coggygria* and clumps of orange-flowered *Hemerocallis* (the old-fashioned *Hemerocallis fulva* 'Flore Pleno' with golden foliage in spring) establish a structure to the beds with groups of 'Frensham' and 'Super Star' roses which produce their red flowers through most of the summer months. Bright blue delphiniums and complimentary orange *Pardalinum* lilies, a colour combination recommended by Miss Jekyll (although she preferred the shorter-stemmed Herring Lily, *Lilium bulbiferum croceum*) flower early, but dark purple *Aconitum napellus*, *Viticella clematis* 'Kermesina', *Polygonum amplexicaule* with bright crimson spikes, also in permanent sites, are out when the 'red' infillers reach their optimum moment. A recent addition and still to get established is a clump of the purple form of *Cimicifuga racemosa*. Plants chosen for their red flowers and striking bronze or red foliage are added at the beginning of May. Dahlias, scarlet and red lobelias with crimson or green leaves, *Begonia* 'Hatton Castle', bronze-leaved scarlet-flowered cannas (*Canna* 'Le Roi Humbert'), scarlet geranium (*Pelargonium* 'General Champonette') and verbenas (both *Verbena* 'Huntsman' and *V.* 'Lawrence Johnston') are bright beside the bronze-purple leaves of the tender New Zealand Cabbage Trees (the purple forms of both *Cordyline australis* and *C. indivisa*). These, in pots, are sunk at intervals through the border to give an exotic tropical atmosphere. This eye-catching scheme, garish on a dull grey day, mellows in bright sunlight; in rain glistening foliage becomes a foil to the rich colours.

THE ANNUAL OR TROPICAL BORDER AT POWIS

Mr Jimmy Hancock, the Head Gardener at POWIS CASTLE, specializes in unusual tender plants which he uses to decorate a wide border under a 6m/20ft rock wall on the first terrace. Groups of large-leaved tropical-looking plants are interwoven with drifts of colourful flowers. Quick-growing woody plants make a good show during a five months' season, and tender perennials and annuals are all combined in this 'mixed' planting scheme. At Powis Mr Hancock has found it possible to leave dahlias in the ground each winter so they become the permanent plant groups around which other plants are rearranged each spring. Unlike more conventional 'bedding-out' arrangements, the effects here do not depend primarily on plants grown annually from seed; instead cuttings are taken, in late summer or autumn, from tender woody shrubs and these, when rooted, are potted on and sheltered from frost during the winter.

Some very floriferous plants have little suitable cutting material until late in the season; cuttings are then placed in a rooting medium and not disturbed until growth begins again in spring, when they can be potted and fed to encourage growth. Other plants, or at least some specimens of each, are dug up and over-wintered under glass and cuttings are taken in early spring when the days lengthen; quickly rooting in heat at this 'growing' time of year, they can still be ready for planting out in April.

During the winter potted up plants will continue to grow but need very little water; if kept dry, most will survive in temperatures below freezing. Mr Hancock makes the point, which is often overlooked, that many of these plants (unlike soft annuals grown from seed in February) can withstand some frost; a few cold nights will not set them back unduly if they have been hardened off before planting out, which can safely take place by the end of April. He reckons that unless the temperature drops to −4°C/24°F, little damage is done. Hybrids of the Mexican

The 'tropical' border at Powis uses large-leaved plants with fuchsias, Nicotiana langsdorfii *and orange-flowered lantanas to give the desired effects.*

fuchsia, *Fuchsia fulgens,* cannot be planted out until the middle or end of May. Most gardeners find that from the end of February until May space for these sorts of plant is a real problem even if they have a greenhouse adequate in size throughout the rest of the year.

At Powis frost drains quickly down the steep terraces and good soil drainage, combined with winter mulches, ensures that the vulnerable crowns and roots of plants do not get frozen. To the eastern end a *Paulownia*, annually cut back in order to get maximum effects from the foliage, is a feature around which are planted drifts of *Fuchsia fulgens* with green-tipped red tubular flowers, yellow *Nicotiana langsdorfii* (grown annually from seed), and scarlet dahlias (left in the ground and covered with a thick mulch in the winter). To the east a clump of azure-blue *Salvia uliginosa* (hardy if mulched) flowers late in the season in front of *Kniphofia* 'C.M. Prichard' (probably correctly *K. rooperi*), with orange-red ovoid heads opening to greenish-yellow. *Iris confusa* with untidy fan-like leaves flowers much earlier in the season. At the back of the border a large clump of cardoons (*Cynara cardunculus*) is both remarkable in spring with its silvery foliage at ground level and striking towards the end of summer with its thistle-like flower-heads.

Moving westwards (as shown in the plan) along the border, a form of *Pericallis lanata* (syn. *Senecio heritieri*) has bright blue flowers; orange- and mauve-flowered *Lantana* (the latter is *Lantana sellowiana*), and a chocolate-brown *Calceolaria banksii* which came from Mount Stewart in Northern Ireland cover the ground in front of other tender fuchsia hybrids. The air is scented with the flowers of Cherry Pie (*Heliotropium peruvianum*). A large *Datura sanguinea*, a clump of blue-flowered *Solanum laciniatum* (with very poisonous orange fruit), *Abutilon* 'Canary Bird' and the variegated form of the grassy *Arundo donax* are farther back nearer the wall, where a white-flowered *Solanum jasminoides* flourishes and survives the winters. *Penstemon* 'Alice Hindley', a garden form of *P. gentianoides*, with lilac flowers for most of the summer, survives most winters.

Farther east along the terrace *Melianthus major*, with large deeply fingered silver leaves, has spread to make a broad sweep behind *Phygelius rectus* 'African Queen' and yellow-flowered *Chrysanthemum maderense* (correctly *Argyranthemum maderense*). Dark blue *Salvia guaranitica*, white *Nicotiana sylvestris* and yellow *N. glauca* make taller accents. The *Melianthus* is hardy but dies back to the ground each winter; it is unlikely to flower at Powis. At the west end of the terrace tender hybrid Speciosa hebes include *Hebe* 'Simon Delaux' and *H.* 'La Seduisante'; both, with bronze leaves and crimson racemes in summer, make rounded bushes. In front of them a group of *Rehmannia glutinosa* with dusky purple flowers is exotic and picks up the red tones of the hebes.

At Powis in late summer Clematis × jackmanii *with velvet purple flowers, grown on a high umbrella-shaped frame, above chelones and aconitums.*

THREE BLUE-AND-YELLOW THEMES

Three borders in three separate National Trust Gardens are designed with a blue-and-yellow flower scheme. TINTINHULL HOUSE in Somerset, ROWALLANE in Northern Ireland and WALLINGTON HALL in Northumberland. All are treated rather differently and ideas from each could very easily be combined to produce yet another variant in planting style and plant types. The soil in the Tintinhull border is alkaline and very dry, especially at the base of the wall at the back. At Rowallane rainfall is 87.5cm/35in, and the soil is acid. At Wallington conditions partly match those of Rowallane with a lime-free soil and rainfall of 74.5cm/29in, but the winters are colder. However, in spite of definite soil differences, the mixed planting in all of these borders could be interchangeable.

The most formal of the individual colour borders at Tintinhull is in the Eagle Court where eighteenth-century brick walls are contemporary with the classical façade of the house. A succession of blue- and yellow-flowering plants grow in the beds at the base of the walls and, in their seasons, curtain the warm walls. The courtyard site is hot and sunny and although walls give some protection there are certain spots where turbulence and funnels of wind do occasionally sweep even the most securely staked plants out of the ground. Lavender hedges grow under a low wall and the main border design is formal in intent. Groups of 'Peace' roses, alternating bushes of lavender and silver-leaved artemisias and spreading clumps of *Agapanthus* make a firm pattern along the front. The rest of the planting is deliberately freer in style to give a more cottage-garden atmosphere to the border.

In March primrose-yellow *Corylopsis pauciflora* opens the flowering season to coincide with a good form of *Euphorbia characias wulfenii* (possibly seedlings of *E. c. w.* 'John Tomlinson') with citron-coloured flower-spikes. The narrow glaucous leaves of this shrubby spurge are decorative all through the year. Tender evergreen

The north wall of the Eagle Court at Tintinhull is planted with lavenders and agapanthus backed by groups of Argyranthemum *'Jamaica Primrose'.*

Ceanothus flower through spring and summer; in spring *Ceanothus* 'Puget Blue', *C.* 'Italian Skies' and *C.* 'Cascade' all flower to accompany groups of the scented yellow tulip 'Mrs Moon' which is planted between architectural clumps of tall bearded irises. Later these bear pale greenish-yellow tinted flowers. The Welsh Poppy (*Meconopsis cambrica*), almost a garden weed, has seeded between their rhizomes and continues the yellow theme for many summer weeks. Both the *Ceanothus* and *Coronilla glauca* are protected in winter with Netlon wrapping; the latter flowers best in spring but may produce flowers all through the summer and autumn. Forms of *Clematis alpina* and *C. macropetala* (including *C. a.* 'Frances Rivis') clamber through the *Ceanothus* and into tall pyramids of *Abutilon vitifolium* and the darker-flowered *A.* × *suntense*, both of which start to flower in May as the clematis finish. The yellow *Rosa* 'Frühlingsgold' and fern-leaved 'Helen Knight' also flower towards the end of May, coinciding with clumps of blue Siberian Iris which are planted along the base of the wall and do well in spite of the dry soil.

By July the silver-leaved Moroccan Broom (*Cytisus battandieri*) produces its deliciously pineapple-scented flowers and lavender – both *Lavandula* 'Hidcote' with violet flowers and the paler English Lavender – are in flower framed against silvery leaves of artemisias. Small catmints (*Nepeta nervosa*) grow at the front edge and Jacob's ladder (*Polemonium caeruleum*) seeds in any remaining bare soil. *Ceanothus* 'Burkwoodii' flowers in August to accompany the intense blue flower-umbels of hardy *Agapanthus* 'Headbourne hybrid', which increase the size of their clumps each year. The pale tender yellow *Argyranthemum* 'Jamaica Primrose' is used for bedding, planted in three equidistant clumps towards the back of the bed; cuttings are taken in August and rooted for the following season. Tobacco Flowers grown from seed are planted out at the end of May in any remaining space; those with lime-green flowers and the species *Nicotiana langsdorfii*, with delicate yellow trumpets, suit the colour theme. By September two clematis are in flower; *C. tangutica* and *C. t.* 'Bill Mackenzie'; both have dangling lemon-peel flowers. A strange tall perennial Tobacco Flower, *Nicotiana glauca*, with attractive grey-green leaves and small yellow flowers borne on 2.4m/8ft stems, survived the recent mild winter of 1987/88; normally in the British Isles it is treated as an annual and grown from seed. Near it another South American plant, the musk-scented *Cestrum parqui* from Chile, flowers in August; it is a sub-shrub in our climate, its woody stems dying to the ground each winter. The last plant to flower is the scrambling groundsel, *Senecio scandens*, which winds itself into one of the spring-flowering *Ceanothus* and bears yellow daisy-flowers through the autumn.

Except for the bushes of silvery artemisia and some clumps of white Regal Lilies (*Lilium regale album*), all plants in this border are chosen for having either blue or yellow flowers. Miss Jekyll reminds a gardener that 'blue' gardens do not have to be planted exclusively with blue flowers: 'they only have to be beautiful'. One of her

In the walled garden at Rowallane a formal element has been introduced with a blue and yellow flower border scheme. Agapanthus flower in front of Hypericum *'Rowallane'.*

The borders at Rowallane have crane's bill geraniums and day-lilies flowering before the agapanthus and hypericum.

recommendations was the use of *Lilium longiflorum* as a foil; this is more tender and would have to be treated as an annual or be grown in pots and sunk in the border, a much more complicated operation. It can be replaced today by the white *regale*.

This is not an easy area to manage; many of the bulbs and rhizomatous irises resent disturbance and do not enjoy the rich feeding which is essential for roses and annuals. Stepping stones set in the earth make it possible to tidy iris leaves after flowering is over.

In the walled garden at ROWALLANE where the weed-infested borders were treated with dazomet a few years ago (see p. 101), a blue-and-yellow border scheme is controlled and formal. It is planned to contrast with the more 'natural' style in which trees, shrubs and shade-loving perennials are planted in the main beds. Paths still divide this garden into a traditional grid pattern, but rare trees and shrubs, originating from when Mr Hugh Armytage Moore used the walled garden as a 'growing-on' nursery for his woodland, are planted where fruit and vegetables were once grown. In full sun, at one end of the garden nearest the house, narrow beds are edged with Victorian patterned tiles and are a

*At Wallington Hall arches covered with yellow roses extend the interest of a border of blue and yellow flowers
mixed with golden-foliaged shrubs.*

decorative feature. The theme is blue and yellow carried through a long season. In spring blue *Muscari* 'Blue Spike' flowers beside mauve aubrieta and taller golden doronicums. Yellow *Allium moly* spreads through the front of the border intermingling with lavender-coloured *Geranium* 'Johnson's Blue'. Later, by July, blue pansies and *Agapanthus* are a foil to yellow-flowered *Hypericum* 'Rowallane' and bushes of silver-leaved *Senecio* 'Sunshine'. Other 'blues' are contributed by penstemons, a rich blue form (unnamed) and the mauve 'Sour Grapes'. Mr Mike Snowden, the Head Gardener, adds some white penstemons and white *Arabis* as a foil to make the blue flowers seem more intense.

Mr Graham Stuart Thomas designed double purple, blue and yellow borders in the walled garden at WALLINGTON HALL in the early 1970s. Backed by yew hedges, narrow beds, sloping slightly to the south, are linked with metal arches clothed with roses and honeysuckles. The planting is mixed; roses, shrubs and the sort of herbaceous plants which seldom need dividing (or much attention) provide the essential backbone of planting, which, with a clear-cut colour scheme, can be kept to a simple pattern or further elaborated with spring bulbs and summer-flowering annuals. In the borders shrubby potentillas, with neat rounded shapes, are not only attractive in summer with green or grey leaves and yellow flowers carried for a very long period, but in winter their arching brown twiggy growth is decorative and gives the border some height. Between them day-lilies, rudbeckias, Golden Rod and the biennial Evening Primrose (*Oenothera biennis*) all contribute their yellow flowers in season; perennial Catmint, the metallic blue thistle (*Eryngium alpinum*), Monkshood (*Aconitum napellus*) and spires of *Veronica virginica* have flowers in contrasting mauves and misty blues. These perennials are all cut to the ground in late autumn, or if other pressure of garden work is important, the Head Gardener, Mr Geoffrey Moon, leaves this tidying until the following March.

COLOUR BEDS AT MOUNT STEWART

At MOUNT STEWART beds in the Italian Garden to the south of the house are in carefully thought-out colour patterns. The soil is acid and moisture-retentive and humidity is, in general, high. Rainfall is 87.5cm/35in but periods of drought are not unknown. Because of its situation on Strangford Lough exceptionally mild winters are normal. Nevertheless many of the plants grown in these beds would thrive in a colder garden and most are not fussy about a more alkaline soil. To east and west groves of tall *Eucalyptus globulus* give wind protection and make a frame for this part of the garden. From the terrace above, a gap in the tree planting permits a view to the Mountains of Mourne in the far distance.

Groups of beds laid out in strict colour patterns as formal as a parterre surround a fountain on either side of the lawn. The planted areas are divided into four sections, each of which is further subdivided into three parts. All follow a definite colour scheme to which both leaves and flower-heads contribute through the summer season. Low hedges of coloured foliage reinforce the colour themes and mark out strong patterns holding the designs together in the required formality. To the east the predominating colours are bright and 'hot'; to the west grey and glaucous foliage sets off flowers in pale and misty colours.

Plans of a section taken from each of the east and west sections of the lawn are included to demonstrate colour and type of plant.

To the east a bed of standard and bush yellow roses ('Whisky Mac' and 'Yellow Pages') is underplanted with scarlet perennial *Potentilla* 'Gibson's Scarlet' and edged with a 45cm/18in hedge of clipped *Erica erigena* 'W. T. Rackliff'.

A companion bed is mainly of perennial plants with creamy-yellow, orange, vermilion and crimson flowers but is given height with golden-leaved elder (*Sambucus racemosa* 'Plumosa Aurea'), which can be pruned back

BARRINGTON COURT
Lily Garden and Lavender Walk

Lily Garden *Summer*

Lavender Walk *Summer*

Permanent Planting

1. *Viburnum tinus*
2. *Potentilla* 'Katherine Dykes'
3. *Lilium pardalinum*
4. *Helenium autumnale* 'Moerheim Beauty'
5. *Helianthemum* 'Wisley Primrose'

Summer Bedding

6. *Dahlia* 'Top Affair'
7. *Nicotiana* 'Lime Green'
8. *Tagetes* 'Paprika'
9. *Antirrhinum* 'Orange Glow'
10. *Marigold* 'Moonshine'
11. *Rudbeckia* 'Irish Eyes'

Winter Bedding

12. Wallflower 'Orange Bedder'
13. Wallflower 'Golden Bedder'
14. Pansy 'Mount Everest'
15. Pansy 'Coronation Gold'
16. Wallflower 'Primrose Monarch'

Permanent Planting

1. *Perovskia atriplicifolia*
2. Shrub Rose 'Penelope'
3. Rose 'Coral Dawn'
4. *Chaenomeles* 'Moerloosei'
5. *Clematis armandii*
6. *Lavandula angustifolia*
7. *Artemisia ludoviciana*
8. *Phlox* – white

Summer Bedding

9. *Cleome hassleriana* 'Pink Queen'
10. *Salvia horminum* 'Bouquet Mixed'
11. Heliotrope 'Marine'
12. *Verbena rigida*
13. Petunia 'Pink Joy'
14. Aster 'Milady Mixed'
15. Ageratum 'Blue Mink'

Winter Bedding

16. Wallflower 'Giant Pink'
17. Wallflower 'Carmine Icing'
18. *Myosotis* 'Royal Blue'
19. Pansy 'Ullswater'

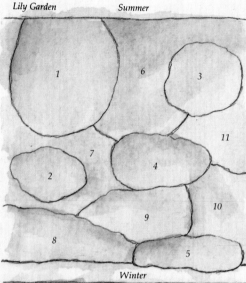
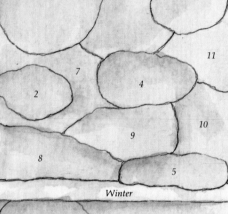
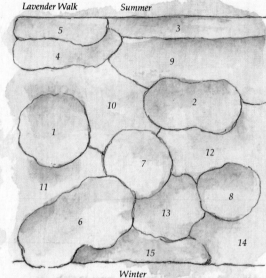

Winter

Winter

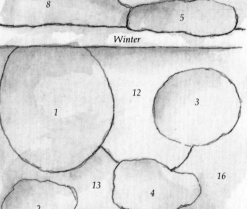
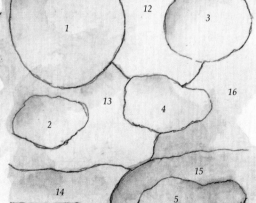
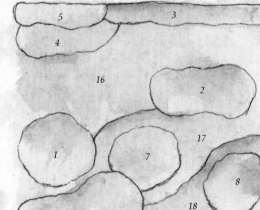

N
↑

DIMENSIONS: *17m × 3.7m (57ft × 12ft)*

DIMENSIONS: *13.5m × 2.5m (45ft × 8ft)*

hard each year to prevent it from dominating other plants. In June a delphinium with cream flowers and tangerine-coloured *Papaver pilosum* are effective with the glowing young foliage of the elder, and penstemons, including *Penstemon* 'Schönholzeri' (syn. *P.* 'Firebird') and *P.* 'Rubicunda', both scarlet-toned, begin to flower. Later the recently introduced yellow form of *Phygelius aequalis* flowers beside a citron-coloured montbretia, cooling contrasting 'hot' colours of bronze-leaved *Lobelia* 'Scarlet Cardinal' and yellow-flowered *Rudbeckia maxima*, both of which need the moisture-retentive soil and high humidity which exists in this garden. The low surrounding hedge is of a dwarf *Berberis, Berberis thunbergii* 'Atropurpurea Nana'.

Planting in the third bed is also mainly of herbaceous perennials with flowers of scarlet, bronze, citron-yellow and apricot with a purple-leaved cotinus (*Cotinus coggygria* 'Royal Purple') as a feature plant. *Monarda didyma* 'Cambridge Scarlet' flowers early beside a dark purple delphinium and the even darker carmine-flowered *Paeonia* 'Monsieur Martin Cahusac', while clumps of strong day-lilies, including *Hemerocallis* 'Stafford' and *H.* 'Burning Daylight' have mahogany-bronze flowers in July. Corms of *Watsonia beatricis* flourish in the mild climate at Mount Stewart and add an exotic note by late summer, flowering between clumps of *Rudbeckia subtomentosa*, with black-eyed yellow daisies, and the brilliant scarlet blooms of *Penstemon* 'Schönholzeri'; the latter flowers from midsummer to October if dead-heads are regularly removed. In gardens with a less favourable climate other watsonias, forms of *Watsonia pyramidata*, mainly with pink or white flowers, can be lifted and stored for the winter. However, *W. beatricis*, with almost evergreen grassy foliage, does not like to be dried off. This bed is edged round with a low hedge of a golden-leaved cultivar of *Thuja occidentalis*.

On the western fringe of the lawn the eucalyptus trees cast light shade over the beds where paler pink, blue and white flower colours predominate, with occasional strong accent given by the magenta-crimson flowers of the tall

At Mount Stewart the Italian garden has definite colour schemes. On one side grey and silver edging plants frame pastel flowers.

Geranium psilostemon in June and July and by bright blue spherical heads of *Agapanthus inapertus pendulus* in August. All the 'reds' here have distinct bluish pigment and none of the flaming almost vermilion touches found in the east beds. The only plants used in both east and west parterres are the purple-leaved cotinus and, round the roses, the same Mediterranean heather, *Erica erigena* 'W. T. Rackliff', is used for a hedge. Standards of the creamy-white rose 'Pascali' give height above 30 bushes of 'Dame Edith Helen', a 1920s Hybrid Tea double pink rose, underplanted with pink-flowering *Potentilla* 'Miss Willmott'. The *Cotinus* is a feature to contrast with silvery-grey foliage of *Artemisia ludoviciana*. Near the *Cotinus*, iris, *Astilbe, Hemerocallis* and *Dicentra* contribute foliage shapes, while mauve and pink flowers from thriving perennials succeed each other through the summer. The white form of Martagon Lily, *Veronica virginica alba* and *Astilbe* 'Bridal Veil' have almost white flower-heads, tinted rather than a pure 'laundry-white', blending gently with the overall colouring. Shining young leaves of the Toad Lily (*Tricyrtis formosana* Stolonifera group) are welcome in spring, and their tall stems bear spotted reddish-mauve flowers in late summer. The glaucous-leaved Jackman's Rue (*Ruta graveolens* 'Jackman's Blue') which make up the surrounding hedge begins to resent the eucalyptus canopy overhead, but its particular foliage contribution is hard to replace with an alternative.

In the third section hedged by grey-leaved *Hebe albicans* planting is dominated by the Californian Tree Poppy (*Romneya coulteri*) with soft greyish-green foliage and papery white flowers. To extend flower colour until the first cold spell pink-flowered *Dahlia* 'Gerrie Hoek' is planted to make a strong group. *Olearia moschata*, a rare shrub, reflects the microclimate at Mount Stewart. With grey almost silvery leaves the bush grows here to a height of 90cm/3ft and as much across and is covered in white daisy-flowers in July.

Different-coloured border phlox and late-flowering Japanese anemones finish the season.

Mr Nigel Marshall, the Head Gardener, writes about the seasonal maintenance of the formal beds:

'AUTUMN AND WINTER WORK
Certain vigorous plants such as *Veronica virginica*, *Geranium psilostemon*, *Hemerocallis*, kniphofias, border phlox and *Campanula lactiflora* need to be lifted and divided approximately every three years or they begin to dominate the various colour combinations and groupings of plants. The foliage is cut down prior to lifting. The ground is dug over, incorporating garden compost and well-rotted farmyard manure. This is also a good time to remove any persistent perennial weeds such as bindweed or couch grass. After digging the ground is well firmed by treading with the feet prior to planting. The plants are then divided, usually with two forks back to back. The divided pieces should have three to four crowns to ensure nice-sized clumps for flowering in the following season.

This is a good opportunity to make any necessary adjustments in the planting plans, altering shapes and relationships of groups. Also by putting plants in different places over a period of years the incidence of 'replant sickness' is lessened. (This applies particularly to roses, which cannot be replanted in the same beds where they have been for many years.) Border phlox also seem to benefit from being moved to a new site every few years.

At this time of year most of the foliage may be cut down and the ground generally tidied up and lightly forked over. However the stems and leaves of tender plants such as fuchsias, penstemons and salvias should not be removed until the spring to help to protect the base of the plants from severe frosts through the winter. In addition bracken or other fern foliage can be worked into the ground round the base of the more tender plants. Cannas, dahlias and any other plants with tubers are best if lifted from the ground and stored in a frost-proof shed over the winter. *Lobelia cardinalis* and its various garden hybrids are also vulnerable and best lifted and 'boxed' up, then placed in a cold frame for the winter, where the foliage is kept dry. These plants, completely hardy in their own habitat where winters are much more severe than in Britain, suffer more from alternating periods of cold weather and wet followed by mild spells which encourage premature growth: further cold will then nip shoots and weaken the plants' constitution. In north-east America their crowns often remain in frozen wet ground all through the winter and emerge healthy in the warmth of spring. The young basal growths of other plants such as delphiniums will be attacked by slugs during any mild spells in the autumn. This may seem unimportant, but often they lay eggs round the crown of the plant and new shoots are ravished in the following spring causing real havoc. Either slug pellets or liquid slug killer should be applied to stop these pests.

SPRING WORK
In the spring work starts when ground conditions allow and any winter tasks still outstanding are completed as soon as possible. The remainder of last year's foliage may also be removed before any young shoots start to emerge as otherwise they may get damaged in the process of cutting back. Some plants such as *Aster amellus* varieties, ornamental grasses and kniphofias are best lifted and divided at this time of year rather than during the autumn. Apply a general garden fertilizer at 70g per square metre/2 oz per square yd at this time of year and lightly fork it in and generally tidy up the soil. This is a good time to apply a mulch of compost or spent mushroom manure before too much growth appears on the plants. In the past mushroom compost was 'lime'-based and would tend to make the soil more alkaline over a period of years so that some nitrogen would have to be added, but the composition of growers' compost now normally does not bring this side-effect.

Opposite the pale border at Mount Stewart, purple and golden foliage shrubs are clipped to make low hedges to enclose beds with orange and red flowers. This represents the 'hot' section of the colour spectrum.

During April and May plants such as fuchsias, lobelias, young penstemons (taken as cuttings the previous season), and salvias can be safely planted out. They will stand the occasional overnight frost if properly hardened off. Dahlias and cannas are best left for a further few weeks until all danger of spring frosts has passed. As growth proceeds certain plants should be either staked or supported with bushy twigs cut to about two-thirds of the expected height of the flower-stems. For staking strong plants such as delphiniums, use 1.5m/5ft bamboo canes, allowing two flower-spikes to each cane. Shoots on delphiniums are best thinned out to give good-quality flower-spikes. This should be done when shoots are about 23cm/9in in length, allowing seven or eight spikes per each established clump. Each stem will need two or three ties before actual flowering time.

SPRAYING OPERATIONS

Herbaceous plants are not often bothered by garden pests. In some areas capsids can be troublesome and will spoil fuchsias, puncturing foliage and stems and preventing flower-buds from opening. One spray with a systemic insecticide should be sufficient control, if applied when foliage growth is well advanced but before any capsid damage is visible. Delphiniums are often subject to mildew attack, especially in areas of high humidity. This can be prevented by spraying with benomyl once or twice in the growing season. If lilies (and some other *Liliaceae*) and peonies are grown watch for *Botrytis*, especially in a wet season as this can ruin the plants. Benomyl will also counteract this, and a systemic insecticide added to the mixture will control the aphids which carry certain virus diseases fatal to lilies in particular.

ROUTINE SUMMER WORK

This consists mainly of removing spent flower-heads on plants to prevent seeding and to allow later flowering. After flowering, forms of *Anthemis* should be cut down to about 15cm/6in to encourage basal growth before the autumn, which is then left on for flower production the following season. August is a good time to lift and divide the bearded iris, *Iris germanica*. This is necessary roughly every five or six years. After lifting incorporate garden compost or well-rotted farmyard manure into the soil and apply a handful of bone-meal. In gardens where the soil is acid add two handfuls of hydrated lime per square metre/yard. When replanting select the strong young rhizomes from around the outside of the old clumps. These should not be buried but planted with the top half above soil level. Heucheras are best if divided and replanted in September rather than in the following spring. Plant the woody rootstock well below soil level to prevent them drying out.

DWARF HEDGES AROUND THE BEDS

Low-growing hedges round the edge of the beds conform with the two distinct colour schemes. At the east end where there are strong flower colours of red, orange, yellow and purple, the hedges are of plum-coloured *Berberis thunbergii* 'Atropurpurea Nana' and a golden-leaved cultivar of *Thuja occidentalis*. To the west where the colouring is much softer, the plants with pink, mauve, lavender, white and cream flowers predominating, the low hedges are of grey-leaved *Hebe albicans* and glaucous *Ruta graveolens* 'Jackman's Blue'. All the hedges are clipped over twice a year, in spring and mid- or late summer to keep them approximately 45cm/18in high and 30cm/12in wide. Even at Mount Stewart there are occasional losses of Rue, which is probably due to the fact that this west end of the south lawn is shaded and overhung by nearby trees (which would have been newly planted when the colour schemes were first devised in the 1930s), especially during the afternoons, making the plants 'drawn' and young stems and foliage soft and susceptible to cold winters. Being a Mediterranean plant, Rue thrives where open exposure to sun will ripen and harden the wood. The cool damp atmosphere experienced in this Irish microclimate encourages excessive growth, and this – combined with wet soil conditions – makes such a plant vulnerable to frost.

There are various other problems associated with these 'colour' beds. In original planting plans bergamot (forms of *Monarda didyma*) were used but did not prove a success in this maritime climate. They suffer from dry spells in summer, and humidity causes mildew. Border phlox, while invaluable for colour display during August, all have to be protected by rabbit netting. Rabbits are a severe trouble but fortunately netting need only be 45cm/18in high and by midsummer is completely hidden by foliage. It is interesting to note that forms with variegated leaves – 'Harlequin' and a new white-flowered cultivar from the USA, 'Mt Fujiyama' – are ignored by the rabbit population and never need protection.

Japanese anemones provide a long season of colour in late summer but are rather invasive. These have to have their roots chopped round with a spade quite frequently to keep them within bounds. It is not advisable to lift them regularly and replant as they take a few years to settle down again after disturbance. *Echinacea purpurea*, with mauve-crimson daisy flowers on strong branching stems, has also not been a success at Mount Stewart. Unfortunately nurserymen usually distribute this plant in autumn but it only does really well if transplanted in spring.

ROSE-BEDS
In the four corner beds of both parterres Hybrid Tea and Floribunda roses are planted to conform with the colour schemes in neighbouring beds. Five standard roses are underplanted with some three dozen of the bush type. These in their turn have groups of low-growing herbaceous potentillas planted beneath them as ground cover. In spring tulips, chosen to give a hint of the colour patterns which come later in the season, provide interest. The rose-beds are surrounded by hedges of shrubby *Erica mediterranea* (now correctly *E. erigena*) 'W.T.Rackliff', which has dark green leaves carried very densely and white flowers with conspicuous brown anthers. The erica is clipped over annually after flowering and the hedging is kept to a height matching the material used round the flower-beds.'

ALL-YEAR COLOUR AT BARRINGTON COURT

BARRINGTON COURT gardens, although attached to a National Trust property, are entirely maintained and run by the Lyle family, who have lived at Barrington Court since 1923. The Lyles created the series of gardens we see today, at first employing Gertrude Jekyll to make plans for planting, but finally using designs by Forbes and Tait, the architectural firm already involved in the restoration of the house. The resulting inner gardens have a strong Jekyllian flavour, with separate areas at their best in succeeding months throughout the summer and colour schemes carefully graded to an overall plan.

Miss Christine Middleton, Head Gardener, writes about the maintenance of borders where, with strict colour themes, annuals are used to extend flowering displays:

'The gardens were planned within existing walls of some old cattleyards. Four flower gardens were designed with quite distinct permanent plants. Summer and winter bedding schemes increase the length of flowering periods over the year. Through the years two distinct colour schemes have predominated in two separate walled enclosures. In one the colouring is hot and bright, mainly in yellow, orange, red, green and white. In the other more subtle tints are used, mainly pink, mauve, blue and white. By limiting colours grown near each other to those closely related in the spectrum, there are no jarring effects.

The colour plan is adhered to each year, but different plants may well be used. It is not intended to make the garden a 'museum piece', planted to a strict design repeated annually, but rather to allow the idea of successful colour combinations to develop further.

SUMMER BEDDING
Against the wall in the Lily Garden the evergreen *Viburnum tinus* flowers in winter and early spring. On the wall the climbing rose 'Dublin Bay' has rich blood red flowers and abundant glossy leaves. Permanent plants include *Lilium pardalinum* with orange-red purple-spotted flowers, *Helenium autumnale* 'Moerheim Beauty' with bronze daisies, the shrubby *Potentilla* 'Katherine Dykes' and in the front plants of *Helianthemum* 'Wisley Primrose' with small grey leaves and pale yellow flowers. Summer bedding plants are *Dahlia* 'Top Affair',

At Barrington Court spring borders are massed with annuals such as wall-flowers, pansies, primulas and forget-me-not all in bright colours to match the azaleas.

Rudbeckia 'Irish Eyes', African Marigolds (*Tagetes erecta* 'Moonshot' and *T.* 'Paprika'), *Antirrhinum* 'Orange Glow' and *Nicotiana* 'Lime Green'. Although essentially this Lily Garden scheme is 'bright', by being confined to a definite range colour clashes are avoided.

The colour scheme in the Lavender Walk is pink, mauve and white, with silvery-grey foliage textures. Permanent plants here are *Clematis armandii*, rose 'Coral Dawn' and *Chaenomeles* 'Moerloosii' on or against the wall, while bushes of English Lavender, the Hybrid Musk rose 'Penelope', *Perovskia atriplicifolia*, *Artemisia ludoviciana* and groups of white border phlox are beside the brick path.

The bedding plants echo the more permanent specimens, extending the range during the summer months. They include

Ageratum 'Blue Mink', *Aster* 'Milady Mixed', *Cleome hassleriana* 'Pink Queen', Heliotrope 'Marine', *Petunia* 'Pink Joy', *Salvia horminum* 'Bouquet Mixed' and *Verbena rigida*.

RAISING OF SUMMER BEDDING
Dahlias can be either potted and started into growth in a cold frame or planted straight into the ground in late April. All other plants are raised in a glasshouse with a minimum temperature of 5°C/40°F. Seed is sown in trays of peat-based seed compost and kept in a propagating case at 10–18°C/50–65°F until germination occurs. Trays are then removed to a glasshouse bench where seedlings are grown on until large enough to be pricked off into John Innes No 1 potting compost; cleomes and Heliotropes are potted into 8cm/3½in pots. Plants are then grown on until large enough to be transferred to cold frames for hardening off before planting out.

Beds are prepared by being forked over, given a dressing of balanced fertilizer and raked after a firm treading. Plants are put in and watered, and slug pellets are scattered near by.

The dahlias will need staking but all the other plants are self-supporting, although the cleomes might need some support if in a wind funnel or exposed position. Hoeing is the only summer task necessary to keep this bedding scheme tidy throughout the summer from May to September. Antirrhinums, dahlias and marigolds will, of course, need regular dead-heading to keep flowering continuous.

WINTER BEDDING
Wallflowers predominate as winter bedding in both areas. Bright yellows and oranges are echoed by white and yellow pansies in the Lily Garden. Pink and richer red tones are used in the Lavender Walk, accompanied by blue pansies and forget-me-nots.

RAISING OF WINTER BEDDING
All seed is sown in drills in open ground in the nursery area at the end of May or beginning of June. The plants are transplanted as soon as they are large enough into open ground in the kitchen garden 23-30cm/9-12in apart with 30cm/12in between rows. They are grown on until the middle of October when they are lifted and moved to their flowering positions. Before the winter plants are bedded out, the beds are forked over with the addition of garden compost and fertilizer. The soil is consolidated and plants put in 23cm/9in apart. They are watered, and slug pellets are scattered near by.'

Summer bedding in the Lily Garden

	raising of bedding plants				bedding out		
plant	sown	germinated	pricked off	outside	planted	distance apart	eventual height	quantity
African marigold	4 Apr	7 Apr	15 Apr	7 May	28 June	23cm (9in)	30cm (12in)	25
Rudbeckia	5 Mar	10 Mar	29 Mar	29 Apr	28 June	30cm (12in)	60cm (2ft)	12
Antirrhinum	8 Feb	17 Feb	15 Mar	15 Apr	28 June	23cm (9in)	30cm (12in)	40
Nicotiana	28 Mar	10 Apr	18 Apr	7 May	28 June	23cm (9in)	60cm (2ft)	25
Tagetes	4 Apr	7 Apr	28 Apr	11 May	28 June	15cm (6in)	23cm (9in)	40
Dahlia	overwintered tubers					90cm (3ft)	135cm (4ft 6in)	3

Summer bedding in the Lavender Walk

	raising of bedding plants				bedding out		
plant	sown	germinated	pricked off	outside	planted	distance apart	eventual height	quantity
Ageratum	5 Mar	9 Mar	7 Apr	7 May	25 June	15cm (6in)	23cm (9in)	25
Aster	28 Mar	30 Mar	18 Apr	7 May	25 June	23cm (9in)	23cm (9in)	30
Cleome hassleriana	15 Mar	22 Mar	5 Apr	28 May	25 June	60cm (2ft)	90cm (3ft)	9
Heliotrope	5 Mar	13 Mar	1 Apr	7 May	25 June	30cm (12in)	30cm (12in)	7
Petunia	19 Feb	26 Feb	15 Mar	15 Apr	25 June	23cm (9in)	23cm (9in)	20
Salvia horminum	28 Mar	31 Mar	7 Apr	28 Apr	25 June	30cm (12in)	45cm (18in)	25
Verbena rigida	overwintered plants					23cm (9in)	45cm (18in)	25

MOUNT STUART
Parterres

N
↑

West Parterre

1. *Cotinus coggygria* 'Royal Purple'
2. *Artemisia ludoviciana*
3. *Anemone* 'Hadspen Abundance'
4. *Geranium psilostemon*
5. *Veronica virginica alba*
6. *Iris* 'Jane Phillips'
7. *Agapanthus inapertus pendulus*
8. *Delphinium* (lilac-pink)
9. *Dicentra spectabilis*
10. *Tricyrtis formosana* Stolonifera group
11. *Astilbe* 'Bridal Veil'
12. *Hemerocallis* 'Pink Damask'
13. *Filipendula purpurea*
14. *Lobelia × vedrariensis*

15. *Salvia* 'East Friesland'
16. *Polemonium foliosissimum*
17. *Romneya coulteri*
18. *Anemome* 'September Charm'
19. *Delphinium* (white)
20. *Dahlia* 'Gerrie Hoek'
21. *Olearia moschata*
22. *Iris* 'White City' with *Allium christophii*
23. *Dictamnus albus*
24. *Phlox paniculata* 'Elizabeth Campbell'
25. *Astilbe* 'Amethyst'
26. *Monarda* 'Prairie Night'
27. Standard Rose 'Pascali'
28. Bush Rose 'Dame Edith Helen' & *Potentilla* 'Miss Willmott'

East Parterre

1. *Lobelia* 'Scarlet Cardinal'
2. *Phygelius aequalis* 'Yellow Trumpet'
3. *Crocosmia* 'Citronella'
4. *Phlox paniculata* 'Harlequin'
5. *Rudbeckia maxima*
6. *Delphinium* (creamy)
7. *Lobelia × vedrariensis*
8. *Crocosmia* 'Carmin Brillant'
9. *Penstemon* 'Schönholzeri'
10. *Phlox paniculata* 'Prince of Orange'
11. *Potentilla recta macrantha*
12. *Inula hookeri*
13. *Penstemon* 'Rubicunda'
14. *Sambucus racemosa* 'Plumosa Aurea'
15. *Papaver pilosum*

16. *Phlox paniculata* 'Red Indian'
17. *Monarda* 'Cambridge Scarlet'
18. *Cotinus coggygria* 'Royal Purple'
19. *Centaurea ruthenica*
20. *Delphinium* (purple)
21. *Watsonia beatricis*
22. *Hemerocallis* 'Stafford'
23. *Rudbeckia subtomentosa*
24. *Heuchera* 'Greenfinch'
25. *Paeonia* 'Monsieur Martin Cahusac'
26. *Hemerocallis* 'Burning Daylight'
27. Rose 'Whisky Mac'
28. Rose 'Yellow Pages' & *Potentilla* 'Gibson's Scarlet'

DIMENSIONS: *3.6m × 3.6m (12ft × 12ft) Small square beds
and 4.5m × 6m (15ft × 20ft) Larger irregular beds*

BASIC METHODS

Making a plan

Even if there is no slavish intention to adhere exactly to a blueprint, it is still useful to put a border plan on paper. Use squared graph paper which is featured in centimetres. It is simplest to use a scale of 1cm to a metre (1 in 100) or 2cm to a metre (1 in 50). First mark in areas of relative sun and shade; then put in the larger plants, trees and large shrubs which have a strong influence on the final design effect. Next shade in the evergreen plants so that the winter 'bones' of the scheme are emphasized. Often there will be plants already *in situ*; these influence further decisions. The next stage is to decide on feature plants, those which give an air of repetition either in a formal rhythm or scattered. These may be plants with a strong natural architectural appearance, those which can be shaped to have an architectural role, or plants with coloured leaves or flowers which set a definite theme to the border. After that plants are added which harmonize with each other and are suitable for their positions, for the whole ambience of the border and the garden in which it is set. If a cottage-garden style is desirable then the composition should remain pictorial, as if it were a flat canvas, trees and bushes give 'weight' and balance but without obvious repetition of effects; all must appear effortlessly casual. Unfortunately this can sometimes be an excuse for both arbitrary and haphazard planting which is not necessarily cottage-garden style.

A semi-circular border at Anglesey Abbey, backed by a beech hedge, is packed with blue, yellow and creamy herbaceous perennials. Dominated by plumed Aruncus *and delphiniums the borders are at their best in mid-summer.*

The plans of the National Trust borders reproduced in this book demonstrate the difference between various styles of planting and types of plants.

Preparation

If a new border is to be made or an old one renovated the first essential is the proper preparation of the soil – digging, cleaning and enriching with organic composts to improve the texture as well as to provide nutrients.

In areas where the ground is waterlogged, it may be necessary to dig out some subsoil and provide freer drainage with stones and gravel. If the garden is new, make certain the builder has left sufficient topsoil on the site. All ground should be dug to a depth of two spits and some bulky organic manure incorporated before any planting begins. It will not be possible completely to dig over a shrub or mixed border once planting of the permanent woody plants has been established; a border with only herbaceous plant material will be dug every few years, either as a whole or in parts.

Where a border is very badly infested with perennial weeds, or to avoid replant sickness for plants such as roses, it is best to undertake the drastic treatment of thoroughly sterilizing the soil of the entire bed. There are no short cuts for this process, but much of the work is basic good sense for any situation: the only extra elements are the use of a sterilizing chemical and the 'sealing' of the ground for a period. The full description of the procedure at ROWALLANE (see p. 100) shows not only how weeds are eradicated but also how the existing herbaceous plants and shrubs in the border are dealt with during this essential exercise.

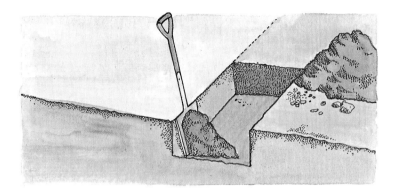

1. Remove the top spit and store on plastic sheet:

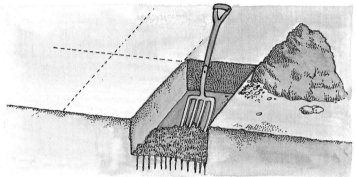

2. Dig and fork over the lower level.

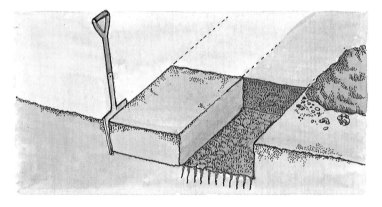

3. Move the top level of the next section on to the first area.

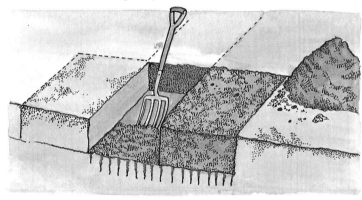

4. Dig the lower surface to end of row, and use first top spit to fill in.

Planting

Even in well-prepared soil, holes should be ample – at least twice the volume of the root-ball. Some extra planting medium – a combination of grit, loam and peat – can be shaken round the plant as the roots are settled in. When planting in spring, a handful of dried organic fertilizer (or slow-release granules) can be added usefully. With most plants (especially those in containers) it is obvious where soil level should be round the stem or crown. Planting too deeply is not uncommon and can lead to collar-rot. Where soil conditions are likely to be on the dry side, make a shallow hollow. Some plants such as peonies and iris should be planted just under the surface of the soil. Tap-rooted plants, such as eryngiums and verbascums, need extra depth for roots.

When moving established plants try to keep as much soil round the roots as possible. Lift gently and place on a plastic sheet and wrap tightly while carrying to the new position where the hole has been previously but only recently prepared. Handle stems and leaves gently; firm in with feet (shrubs) and hands (perennials and annuals), but not enough to compact soil. Prune back all woody plants to prevent vulnerability to winds in the period before roots can adequately anchor the plant; stake if necessary.

When planting in groups of two, three, five or whatever, arranging all the plants on the surface of the soil before planting the first one makes all the difference to the aesthetic effects later on, as well as ensuring more or less equal spacing to allow plants to thrive. This may be difficult with a tray of 50 annuals; in this case place the first five or so into a pleasing arrangement and then plant in position, having established average distances between each plant.

Evergreen shrubs are best planted either in September when the soil is still warm and roots can get established before frosts and chilling winds bring dehydration, or in spring with warm weather ahead. Deciduous shrubs and roses can be planted most appropriately during the winter if the weather and conditions are suitable. If the ground is hard it is far better to store plants in some frost-free place (even those, such as roses, which are often bare-rooted) rather than in containers. Container-grown shrubs and all other plants can also be planted in spring, summer and autumn; in periods of drought afterwards they should be watered. Beware of specimens which have been insufficiently established in containers; they will fall or pull out when the pot is tipped up without any ball of soil. Equally those too well established will have become root-bound and may never thrive. In the latter case it is best to cut off some of the root and repot in a larger container to allow a new fibrous root system to form before planting them out. Large shrubs and small trees may have had many of the small fibrous roots cut off in order to fit them in the restricted space of a container; they look good but may never form a new root system.

Plants obtained from reputable nurseries should have none of these problems; unfortunately some garden centres are places only for selling and lack facilities and labour for potting on. Those who grow their own plants from cuttings or seed discover quickly how frequently plants need upgrading to a larger-sized container – especially in warm growing weather.

Feeding and watering

The maintenance tasks through the year include ensuring that plants have sufficient food and water. If plants are healthy and well-fed they are far less likely to develop disease. Organic fertilizers such as farmyard manure seldom provide sufficient nutrients on their own; the mulches, applied in autumn when the soil is warm or in spring to conserve moisture before the soil dries out, have little feed value but they do improve the texture of the soil and make it possible for plants to take up nutrients provided in an artificial form. Any well-balanced fertilizer can be used; those with a high nitrogen content encourage foliage growth.

It is worth considering installing some sort of watering system. If tall perennials are part of the scheme it is seldom possible to use overhead sprays after the end of May as the soft stems and foliage will be beaten down; instead, trickle hoses with perforations can be laid at the highest point in the back or in the centre of the bed. For most other borders sprays and conveniently sited standpipes should be provided.

Routine maintenance

After the border has been planned and planted there are routine tasks through a gardening year. In September and October and in March and April herbaceous plants are being divided and shuffled in their places. Mulches are applied in late autumn after herbaceous plants have been cut down, and again in spring as the ground warms up. In spring soil panned by winter rains needs cultivating with a fork to let in air and improve the appearance before the mulch is added round the base of shrubs and round the crowns of herbaceous plants. The young growths of herbaceous plants are easily rooted in spring; with four or five growing months ahead in which to make a healthy root system, they can be planted in permanent sites in September. In May perennials such as delphiniums, thalictrums, *Anthemis*, achilleas and galegas need staking

Delphinium stems need individual staking and tying: these must be firm while allowing some movement.

with beech or hazel twigs or with metal supports; the supports should be set at approximately two-thirds of the ultimate height each plant will reach. In a few weeks these are no longer visible. Other plants such as tall crambes and verbascums need strong stakes and twine. By the beginning of May dahlias need similar treatment to protect their brittle stems. At NYMANS even the annuals are staked when they are set in position at the end of May.

By June dead-heading of the early-flowering plants begins; this remains one of the most pressing summer tasks. Many plants which will not flower again in this season will produce attractive new mounds of foliage if cut back severely after flowering is over; this characteristic makes alchemilla, catmints and hardy cranesbill geraniums valuable assets in any border. Most bush roses and some of the modern shrub roses and dahlias will flower all summer if the dead-heads are regularly removed; other plants such as penstemons and herbaceous potentillas have bursts of flowering. Shrubs such as deutzias, spiraeas and kolkwitzias should have their flowering branches cut back and any untidy new growth shaped. In the following year they will flower on woody shoots produced in the second half of the current summer. Shrubs which flower later in the season, such as most buddlejas and hydrangeas, do not receive attention until winter or early spring. As plants are cut back they will

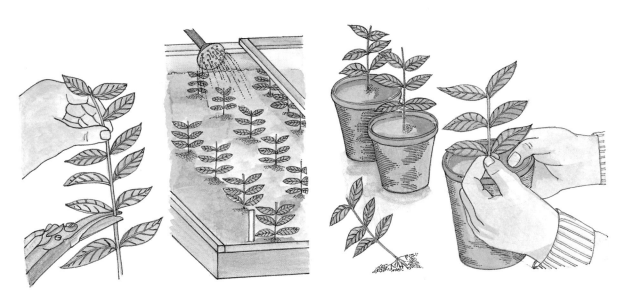

Using very sharp secateurs, or preferably a knife, cut below nodes of half-ripe stems, dust base of stem in rooting compound containing fungicide, and place in rooting medium on a bench or in pots out of direct sunlight. Keep atmosphere moist to prevent dehydration and leave to root.

Most plants can be treated quite roughly when they need dividing but forks and fingers to disentangle roots are as necessary as a sharp knife. For large plants two forks, back to back, should be used for dividing.

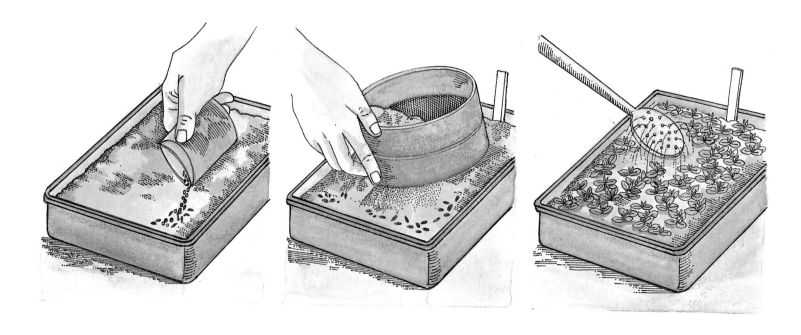

Sow seeds well apart in damp compost (if very fine seed mix with sand to get an even spread) and use a sieve to cover with a little soil. Do not water until seeds are well grown. Prick off into larger trays.

benefit from extra feeding: in small areas fertilizers in liquid forms can be used, in large borders slow-release pellets scattered earlier in the season are invaluable.

In August cuttings to be rooted for use in the following season are taken of plants such as penstemons and other doubtfully hardy plants. After rooting they can be kept in a frost-free greenhouse or cold frame until the spring; those which do not make roots until September can be left in the rooting medium until the spring before being potted up individually. By September it is possible to start moving and dividing suitable herbaceous plants. A list below indicates those which can be split and replanted at this time of year. Some gardeners like to postpone all division (and even cutting down) until the following spring; in cold gardens this may be wise, but pressure of other spring work in the garden is always a problem.

Penstemon cuttings are taken in late summer and rooted and potted on or before October. Store in frames over winter.

Compost

Mr Graham Kendall, the Head Gardener at MONTACUTE HOUSE, describes his method of making compost:

'Most National Trust gardens have been cultivated for a very long time, and Montacute has been a garden for three and a half centuries. As soils inevitably become leached and tired, nutrients have to be added either by using proprietary fertilizers or by the application of manures and composts, which have the additional benefit of improving soil structure.

We do use proprietary fertilizers because they are quick and easy to apply. We also prepare our own compost, which we use mainly as a mulch. Time, however, prohibits too scientific an approach to the preparation of our heap, and lack of availability of plant material limits its quality. The bulk of our material consists of grass cuttings through the growing season and fallen leaves gathered in the autumn. We acquire these in large enough quantities to swamp other ingredients, which include fibrous rooted weeds – hopefully with some soil still attached – and bonfire ash. The latter, while containing potash, is of more dubious benefit and is composted as a convenient method of disposal.

A limited range of ingredients can still produce a very useful compost. Grass cuttings are rich in nitrogen, phosphate and

Dahlia cuttings can be taken in spring when old dahlia tubers first shoot in a heated greenhouse.

potassium as well as other nutrients. Leaf litter, especially beech leaves, which are plentiful here, has virtually no nutrient value, except for calcium which is retained in the leaf skeleton. This skeleton adds fibre to the heap, which forms humus. Humus is a black colloid material which coats individual soil particles. On light soils it will hold the particles together and retain water. On heavy soils it reduces stickiness and makes soil more friable.

Our heap is started in early spring, on forked-over earth. It is contained in a bay constructed of corrugated iron sheets. We use compost left over from the previous year as an activator. As we are constantly adding to it, we do not cover the heap, although it would be beneficial to do so through the winter to keep heat in and prevent the leaching of nutrients.

The more often a heap can be turned the better, especially when using large amounts of grass clippings which tend to stick in one soggy mass. A more open structure allows air into the heap, encouraging the right organisms for decomposition. Moisture is also necessary and, because of the amount of grass used, our heap seldom dries out. We make our heap wide and low and this increases the surface area for absorbing rainfall. Lime is often added to a heap to prevent acidity, but as the garden at Montacute stands on limey soil we have not found this necessary. The compost from the first year is ready to use in the spring of the second, and is put on as soon as the soil is warm enough to accept the mulch.

CLEANING THE HERBACEOUS BORDERS AT ROWALLANE

During the early days when the garden at ROWALLANE was being planted by Mr Hugh Armytage Moore, the walled garden was still partly used for kitchen produce but also served as a nursery area for growing on young plants before they were found a place in the woodland garden. As the main woodland developed, the walls and borders within this garden gradually became the permanent sites for ornamentals. Mr Mike Snowden, the Head Gardener at Rowallane, writes about the programme of eradicating weeds in these borders:

'Over many years the walled garden, planted with trees, shrubs, shrub roses and herbaceous plants, became infested with perennial weed, particularly Ground Elder and bindweed, which would have been brought in with leaf-mould and unclean compost. It is an impossible task to try and eradicate those kinds of weeds while keeping all the plants *in situ*, as the roots of the weeds become entangled with those of the ornamentals.

It was therefore necessary to take out all the herbaceous material. We decided to tackle a given area of the garden each year, over a four- or five-year period. This was done for a number of reasons, and partly because other more urgent work in the garden absorbed much of the time of the staff. By doing the work of restoration in stages, less nursery area for temporary storage of plants was needed. Finally, and perhaps most importantly, it is not possible to present a totally denuded garden to visitors, although, in fact, the majority show considerable interest in the work we do, and an explanation of 'work in progress' is posted on our noticeboard.

The method of cleaning involved lifting all herbaceous plants, spraying, cultivating and sterilizing the soil.

The clumps of perennials are labelled during the growing season. Once they are dormant, vigorous sections of each are lifted, divided and washed. Great care is taken to ensure all pieces of weed root are removed. The newly cleaned pieces are lined out and carefully labelled in the nursery beds. Bulbs are dug up as they begin to show. The parts of the plants not needed for the future replanting scheme are just left in the ground. It is possible to lift plants and to keep them in a clamp of leaf-mould until a spell of wet weather allows adequate time for washing and cleaning them.

In the beds the remaining plants and leaves are allowed to develop until foliage is reasonably mature. They are then sprayed all over' with glyphosate, using a hooded sprayer to prevent 'drift' and possible damage to adjacent shrubs and lawn areas. An explanation to visitors is essential at this time: one visitor could not understand why we had such localized frost damage. Ground Elder is very resilient and almost always reappears and needs a second application of the spray. As the leaves wither there is a temptation to remove the unsightly foliage: this must be resisted, as glyphosate is a translocated herbicide, and to ensure full penetration throughout the system of the plant, leaves must remain until the plant is totally dead. Then all the surface debris is removed and burnt.

The bed is now trench dug; all roots are removed and also burnt. At this stage as digging progresses a vertical wall of polythene is placed around trees or shrubs that remain in the bed and are part of the permanent planting scheme. The polythene should be at least 30cm/12in deep and should be round the outer rim of the shrub's canopy so that none of the small fibrous roots will be affected by the chemical which is to sterilize the soil. Care must be taken not to damage the roots, particularly with grafted plants, as this will result in suckers later. Compost is also dug in at this stage.

The next move is the application of dazomet, a soil sterilant in the form of fine granules. This, when incorporated in the soil, will break down with moisture to release gases, which circulate through the soil structure killing pests, soil fungi etc. The soil temperature must be high and the gas must be trapped within the soil. To ensure this we work the granules into the top 15cm/6in of soil, leaving the soil loose in structure but with a level surface.

The granules are added to a stretch of soil a few feet at a time, and a film of polythene is rolled out over the soil almost at once, trapping the gases. The polythene is held tight against the soil surface, and is secured along the edges with planks or heavy fencing posts, which are also laid at intervals along the surface to prevent the wind getting under the sheet and lifting it. A good wide overlap is made when a sheet has to be joined, in order to ensure a continuous airtight film. This work is done in the opposite direction to the earlier digging programme to prevent the soil becoming higher at one end, which would happen if always worked in the same rotation. At the points where trees and shrubs are still in their places in the bed the sheet is cut and folded back to the vertical polythene wall which protects the root system and firmly secured. The surface round the plants is left exposed so no gas can be trapped in the soil.

After the whole bed has been treated and covered it is left for four or five weeks. No harm results from leaving it longer, so the film of polythene can be removed when the weather is dry or the work programme permits a return to the job. After the sheet is removed the bed is left exposed for several days to allow the gases to escape. The surface is then lightly forked through to make sure all the gas has gone. A further week is allowed before replanting. Plants from the nursery area are again carefully examined for any residual weed roots in their soil.

Under the permanent trees and shrubs some perennial weed will reappear; this is treated once again with glyphosate.

The whole operation has been very successful with us. The first border to be completed is now well established and relatively weed-free. One weed we have found a problem is Creeping Sow-thistle not because of its resistance, but because at the recommended rate of application of glyphosate, the foliage is burnt off before translocation into the root system has taken place completely. Recently we have found that spot treatment at a lower rate of dilution delays burning off and appears successful.'

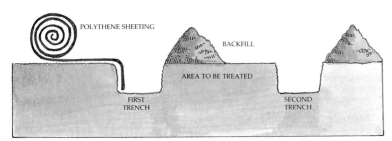
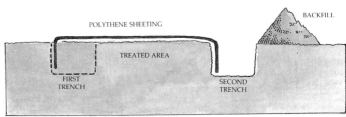

Airtight polythene is rolled over the soil and sealed as the chemical is incorporated.

APPENDICES

Plenty of books provide good descriptions of plants and lengthy and thorough advice for cultivation; there seem few which provide a quick shorthand guide to management. When planning a border, prediction of future timing of maintenance jobs seems essential; it is also vital, besides planning for pleasing juxtaposition of colours and shapes, to put plants together which need the same sort of treatment; if they need dividing up after the same number of years so much the better. The following lists summarize the most important plants in each of the different types useful in borders and provide some brief notes to aid in their successful management. They are intended as a quick *aide-mémoire* for helping to plan plant associations. It surprises me, as I make the lists, how many good traditional plants will continue to flower year after year without much attention. Ground-cover plants do not need regular division although, in some cases, flowering performance will be less as plants mat together.

Appendix A
INDISPENSABLE HARDY BORDER PERENNIALS

Acanthus leave to establish – curb with spade

Achillea division or soft-cuttings in spring – three years

Aconitum division in autumn – rich feeders – partial shade – three years

Alchemilla mollis spreads rapidly – cut off flowering heads to prevent seeding

Alstroemeria once established leave in position – curb with spade

Anemone (hybrid Japanese) once established, leave

Anthemis short-lived – cuttings in autumn – twig supports

Artemisia lactiflora self-supporting – seven or eight years

Artemisia ('silvers') good drainage and sun – frequent propagation from cuttings

Aruncus dioicus foliage and flower value – division infrequent

Aster fleshy-rooted forms: divide in autumn – more woody types: cuttings in spring

Baptisia australis leave undisturbed – increase from seed

Campanula frequent division from named cultivars – or seed from species

Centaurea leave undisturbed

Coreopsis verticillata rich soil – leave to establish – divide in spring if plants required

Clematis recta stake well in May – split every six or seven years – rich soil

Crambe cordifolia foliage and architectural – seed or division autumn or spring when necessary

Crocosmia spiky foliage – spring division when necessary

Cynara scolymus silver foliage – give winter protection to crowns – divide every five years

Delphinium rich feeders – staking – split every four years in spring

Echinops spreader – curb with spade

Eryngium poor soil – full sun – split in spring

Eupatorium purpureum **'Atropurpureum'** pinkish leaves – divide in spring every five years

Euphorbia leave spreaders undisturbed – increase sun-lovers from cuttings or seed

Galega *G. orientalis* is invasive – seldom needs division – best split up in spring – staking in May

Geranium division but rarely

Grasses leave to establish as large clumps but can be invasive

Gypsophila leave undisturbed or cuttings to increase stock

Helenium basic border daisies – divide every six years

Hemerocallis split only when necessary – autumn or spring

Hosta divide with spade – autumn or spring

Kirengeshoma palmata moist acid soil – divide infrequently

Kniphofia choice for long flowering period – architectural leaves and flower-spikes – do not disturb fleshy root system

Ligularia interesting leaf forms – damp soil – division in spring

Limonium latifolium root cuttings if necessary – resent disturbance

Lobelia cardinalis hybrids and *L.* × *vedrariensis* bronze leaves – rich moist soil – protection in winter – divide in autumn and spring – but pot in frame until in growth

Lupinus not for lime soil – no rich feeding – increase from cuttings in spring – renew every three or four years

Lychnis chalcedonica divide infrequently, in autumn

Macleaya cordata foliage – spreader – control with spade – move in autumn or spring

Monarda rich moist soil – division of crowns in spring in alternate years

Osteospermum jucundum autumn cuttings

Paeonia leave undisturbed – move, if necessary, in August

Papaver orientale twiggy supports – leave undisturbed – root cuttings

Phlox no staking required – rich moist soil – divide every three years

Polemonium no staking – sun

Polygonatum leave undisturbed – shade – move in autumn

Rheum palmatum architectural leaves – green and purple – division in spring

Rodgersia foliage for waterside – division in spring

Rudbeckia rich soil – divide every three years – autumn or spring

Salvia guarantica hardier than expected – rich soil – leave undisturbed – cuttings in autumn

S. superba stake with twigs in May – seldom needs splitting – division in spring

Sedum full sun – not fussy about soil – easily divided at any time

Sisyrinchium small iris-like leaves – allow to seed – short-lived – full sun

× *Solidaster* bigeneric hybrid – slow spreader – divide clumps every five years – autumn or spring

Thalictrum resents disturbance – hardly needs staking

Verbascum architectural – full sun – rich soil – seed from species or root cuttings in February from named cultivars – many are biennials

Verbena bonariensis half-hardy but prolific seeder

Viola cornuta cut down in June after flowering – divide every three years and enrich soil

Zauschneria californica (now correctly *Epilobium canum angustifolium*) grey-leaved – sun and good drainage – cuttings of new shoots in spring – only need renewing if rich soil

Appendix B
BEST ANNUALS, BIENNIALS AND HALF-HARDY PLANTS FOR USE IN BORDERS

Agastache often hardy – flowers from seed in season

Argyranthemum daisies – cuttings in autumn – over-winter in greenhouse

Canna decorative leaves – rich feeders – store rhizomes frost-free over winter

Cleome seed each February under glass

Dahlia rich soil – no frost – store tubers – cuttings in spring to increase stock

Felicia tender woody – cuttings in autumn – overwinter in greenhouse

Myosotis biennial – sow each July for spring-flowering

Nicotiana seed each February under glass

Nigella allow to self-seed or sow under glass

Onopordon biennial silver-leaved thistle – seed

Osteospermum ecklonis quick growing tender shrub – cuttings in late summer

Penstemon cuttings in autumn – overwinter in frames

Perilla frutescens purple leaves – seed in February under glass – harden off before planting after frosts

Ricinus comunis purple-leaved form – seed in heated house in February or April in cold frame

Salvia (red and blue-flowered) seed or cuttings in late summer

Verbascum biennials – seed

Verbena (many) propagate from autumn cuttings and seed in February

Appendix C
SMALL PLANTS FOR GROUND COVER
(DIVIDE IN AUTUMN OR SPRING)

Ajuga reptans sun or shade – division

Alchemilla mollis sun or shade – seed

Brunnera macrophylla shade

Cerastium tomentosum full sun - division

Dicentra allow to spread – sun or shade

Epimedium spreading cover – sun or shade – division in spring

Galium ordoratum (Asperula odorata) allow to spread

Geranium (various) division

Heucherella 'Palace Purple' foliage – division

Hypericum calycinum shade – splitting

Lamium maculatum sun – seed or division

Symphoricarpos suckering bushes – autumn colour and fruits

Symphytum grandiflorum division – invasive – total ground cover in sun or shade

Rubus tricolor division – invasive – total ground cover

Tellima shade – division

Tiarella cordifolia shade – division

Vinca sun or shade – division – total ground cover

Viola sun or shade – division or seed

Waldsteinia ternata sun or shade – division

Appendix D
SHRUBS CONTRIBUTING FLOWERS OR FOLIAGE TO THE SHRUB OR MIXED BORDER

Aralia elata variegated leaf forms – architectural shape

Ballota pseudodictamnus grey-leaved for full sun

Berberis good purple-leaved and grey-leaved forms

Buddleja many – particularly useful as needs to be cut back annually

Caryopteris annual April hard pruning – similar to Bush Roses

Choisya ternata evergreen – scented white flowers

Ceanothus wall or prostrate shrubs – tender – full sun

Cistus summer-flowering – hot sun – poor soil

Clematis to scramble through shrubs

Cornus particularly good variegated leaf forms of *Cornus alba* – coloured bark

Corylopsis spring-flowering

Corylus good purple-leaved forms of hazel

Cotinus various green and purple-leaved forms – 'smoke-bush' flower

Cotoneaster architectural shapes – fruit

Cytisus early-flowering brooms

Deutzia graceful shapes – white and pink flowers

Erica ground-cover – winter flowers

Escallonia evergreen – pendulous or upright

Fatsia japonica evergreen – architectural large leaves – late-summer flowers

Hamamelis early spring – prefers acid soil – semi-shade

Hebe evergreen – full sun – summer-flowering

Helichrysum silver or grey leaves – full sun

Hydrangea semi-shade

Hypericum semi-shade

Ilex architectural shapes – green/variegated/golden leaves – slow-growing

Juniperus architectural fastigiate or creeping prostrate for ground cover

Kolkwitzia amabilis spreading large shrub – pink flowers – full sun

Lavandula evergreen grey-green leaves – poor soil – full sun

Leptospermum evergreen silvery leaves – tender

Ligustrum evergreen – golden and silver variegated leaves

Lonicera bushes or twining climbers

Magnolia smaller forms for mixed borders

Mahonia evergreen – spring-flowering

Olearia tender – foliage – daisy bushes

Osmanthus evergreen – trim to architectural shapes

Philadelphus different species flower over long period – scented – golden/variegated leaves

Phillyrea evergreen – trim to architectural shapes

Phlomis grey-leaved – sunny borders

Phygelius sub-shrub – full sun

Physocarpus opulifolius **'Luteus'** golden leaf keeping colour in shade

Potentilla neat compact-shaped bushes – summer-flowerers

Prunus purple-leaved forms as well as flowers

Robinia pseudoacacia **'Frisia'** golden leaves

R.p. **'Umbraculifera'** mop-headed shape

Romneya grey-leaved poppy-flowers for full sun

Rosa shrub and bush roses – flower, foliage and fruit

Rosmarinus aromatic leaves – full sun – poor soil

Salix can be trimmed to architectural shapes

Sambucus gold, purple and laciniate leaf forms – need fierce pruning

Santolina aromatic leaves – grey/silver/green – hot sun – trim in spring

Skimmia evergreen – compact – fruit

Sorbus mainly for foliage – late-summer fruit

Spiraea spring- and summer-flowerers

Symphoricarpos green-leaved and golden-variegated suckering bushes – ground cover and fruits

Syringa scented – early summer

Viburnum evergreen and deciduous – spreading and upright shapes – can be trained to mop-heads – with flower and fruit – autumn colour

Weigela variegated and bronzish-purple leaf forms

Appendix E

BULBS, CORMS AND RHIZOMES SUITABLE FOR BORDER ASSOCIATION
(NOT INCLUDING BULBS SUITABLE FOR NATURALIZING)

Allium sun

Anemone apennina, A. blanda, A. nemorosa light shade – deciduous shrubs

Arum foliage – half-shade under deciduous shrubs

Brodiaea full sun – good drainage

Camassia sun

Chionodoxa half-shade under deciduous shrubs

Corydalis sun or shade

Cyclamen shade of deciduous shrubs

Dodecatheon semi-shade

Erythronium moist – light shade of deciduous shrubs

Fritillaria sun or half-shade

Galanthus shade

Galtonia sun

Iris **(Bearded)** architectural leaves – messy after midsummer – split rhizomes July/August – sun and good drainage

Iris (especially *I. sibirica* and *I. orientalis*) useful back of border – divide after flowering every four years

Leucojum shade or sun

Lilium light shade, except for *Lilium candidum*

Muscari sun – invasive

Scilla sun or shade

Trillium light shade – acid soil

Tulipa sun except for *T. sylvestris* – light shade

BORDER FEATURES IN TRUST GARDENS

Note: This list indicates National Trust, and National Trust for Scotland gardens where borders discussed in this book may be seen: it is not a comprehensive listing of every type of feature in these gardens. Opening times: Trust properties are open between April and October, but visitors are advised to telephone in advance of a visit to check times. Opening times can also be found in *The National Trust Handbook*.

Acorn Bank Garden *Penrith, Cumbria (NT regional office (05394) 33883)*
Mixed border, Rose border.

Anglesey Abbey *Lode, Cambridge, Cambridgeshire (0223) 811200*
Herbaceous border – summer

Ardress House *64 Ardress Rd, Portadown, Co Armagh (0762) 851236*
Mixed border

Arlington Court *Arlington, nr Barnstaple, Devon (027 182) 296*
Herbaceous border

Barrington Court *nr Ilminster, Yeovil, Somerset (0460) 41480*
Mixed border

Blickling Hall *Blickling, Norwich, Norfolk (0263) 733084*
Herbaceous borders

Buscot Park *Farringdon, Oxfordshire (0367) 20786*
Shrub border

Bodnant *Tal-y-Cafn, Colwyn Bay, Gwynedd (0492) 650460 (during office hours)*
Herbaceous borders

Castle Drogo *Drewsteignton, Devon (06473) 3306*
Herbaceous border – summer

Castle Ward *Strangford, Downpatrick, Co Down (039 686) 204*
Mixed borders

Charlecote Park *Wellesbourne, Warwick, Warwickshire (0789) 840277*
Mixed borders

Chartwell *Westerham, Kent (0732) 866368*
Rose Border (mixed)

Clandon Park *West Clandon, Guildford, Surrey (0483) 222482*
Mixed border

Clevedon Court *Clevedon, Avon (0272) 872257*
Mixed border

Cliveden *Taplow, Maidenhead, Berkshire (06286) 5069*
Herbaceous, Mixed borders

Cotehele *St Dominick, nr Saltash, Cornwall (0579) 50434*
Herbaceous, Mixed borders

The Courts *Holt, Trowbridge, Wiltshire (0225) 782340*
Mixed borders

Crathes Castle *Banchory, Grampian (033044) 525*
Herbaceous border

Dunham Massey *Altrincham, Cheshire (061 941) 1025*
Mixed borders

East Riddlesden Hall *Bradford Rd, Keighley, West Yorkshire (0535) 607075*
Mixed borders

Falkland Palace *Falkland, Fife (0337) 57397*
Herbaceous border

Farnborough Hall *Banbury, Oxfordshire (NT regional office (0684) 850051)*
Herbaceous border

Felbrigg Hall *Norwich, Norfolk (02635) 444*
Shrub borders

Glendurgan *Helford River, Mawnan Smith, nr Falmouth, Cornwall (0208) 4281*
Mixed borders

Greys Courts *Rotherfield Greys, Henley-on-Thames, Oxfordshire (049 17) 529*
Mixed borders

Gunby Hall *Gunby, nr Spilsby, Lincolnshire (NT regional office (0909) 486411*
Mixed border, Herbaceous border, Rose border

Hardwick Hall *Doe Lea, Chesterfield, Derbyshire (0246) 850430*
Mixed borders, Rose border

Hidcote Manor Garden *Chipping Campden, Gloucestershire (0386) 438 333*
Mixed borders

Hill Top *at Near Sawrey, Ambleside, Cumbria (09666) 269*
Mixed borders

Ickworth *The Rotunda, Horringer, Bury St Edmunds, Suffolk (028 488) 270*
Mixed borders

Killerton *Broadclyst, Exeter, Devon*
(0392) 881345
Herbaceous border

Knightshayes Court *Bolham, Tiverton, Devon*
(0884) 254665
Mixed border

Montacute House *Montacute, Somerset*
(0935) 823289
Mixed border, Rose border

Mottisfont Abbey *Mottisfont, nr Romsey,*
Hampshire (0794) 40757
Rose borders, Mixed borders

Mount Stewart House *Newtownards, Co*
Down (024 774) 387
Mixed border

Nymans *Handcross nr Haywards Heath, West*
Sussex (0444) 400321
Summer annuals border, Shrub rose border

Ormesby Hall *Ormesby, Middlesbrough,*
Cleveland (0642) 324188
Mixed borders

Overbecks *Sharpitor, Salcombe, Devon*
(054 884) 2893
Mixed borders

Oxburgh Hall *Oxborough nr King's Lynn,*
Norfolk (036 621) 258
Herbaceous border

Packwood House *Lapworth, Solihull,*
Warwickshire (056 43) 2024
Herbaceous borders

Peckover House *North Brink, Wisbech,*
Cambridgeshire (0945) 583463
Herbaceous border, Mixed border, Ribbon
border

Polesden Lacey *nr Dorking, Surrey*
(0372) 58203
Summer border, peony borders

Powis Castle *Welshpool, Powys (0938) 4336*
(during office hours)
Mixed border, annual/tropical border,
autumn flowering border

Rowallane Garden *Ballynahinch, Co Down*
(0238) 510131
Mixed borders

Shugborough *Milford, nr Stafford,*
Staffordshire (0889) 881388
Rose borders

Sissinghurst Castle Garden *Sissinghurst, nr*
Cranbrook, Kent (0580) 712850
Mixed borders

Sizergh Castle *nr Kendal, Cumbria*
(053 95) 60070
Herbaceous foliage border

Snowshill Manor *nr Broadway,*
Gloucestershire (0386) 852410
Mixed borders

Springhill *20 Springhill Rd, Moneymore,*
Magherafelt, Co Londonderry (06487) 48210
Mixed borders

Standen *East Grinstead, West Sussex*
(0342) 23029
Herbaceous, Mixed Borders

Tintinhull House *nr Yeovil, Somerset (NT*
regional office (0747) 840224)
Shrub border, Mixed border

Trelissick Garden *Feock, nr Truro, Cornwall*
(0872) 862090
Mixed borders

Trengwainton Garden *nr Penzance, Cornwall*
(0736) 63021
Mixed borders

Trerice *St Newlyn East, nr Newquay, Cornwall*
(0637) 875404
Mixed colour-schemed borders

Uppark *South Harting, Petersfield, Hampshire*
(073) 085 317
Mixed border

Upton House *Banbury, Oxfordshire*
(029587) 266
Mixed border including Aster border

The Vyne *Sherborne St John, Basingstoke,*
Hampshire (0256) 881337
Herbaceous border

Wakehurst Place Garden *Ardingly, Haywards*
Heath, West Sussex (0444) 892701
Mixed border, Herbaceous border, Monocot
border

Wallington *Cambo, Morpeth, Northumberland*
(067074) 283
Blue and yellow mixed border

Westbury Court *Westbury-on-Severn,*
Gloucestershire (045276) 461
Mixed borders

West Green House *Hartley Wintney,*
Basingstoke, Hampshire (NT regional office
(0372) 53401)
Mixed borders

HORTICULTURAL SOCIETIES

British Hosta and Hemerocallis Society
Hon. Sec., R. Bowden, Cleave House,
Sticklepath, Okehampton, Devon EX20 2NN

The Cottage Garden Society
The Correspondence Secretary, Pat Taylor,
Old Hall Cottage, Pump Lane, Churton,
Chester, Cheshire CH3 6LR

Delphinium Society
V. Labati, 143 Victoria Road, Emmer Green,
Caversham, Reading, Berkshire RG4 8RA

Hardy Plant Society
Mrs. J. Sambrook, 214 Ruxley Lane,
West Ewell, Surrey KT17 9EU

Irish Garden Plant Society
Reg Maxwell, 241 Cavehill Road, Belfast 15
Northern Ireland

Lily Group of the Royal Horticultural Society
Mrs A. C. Dadd, 21 Embrook Road,
Wokingham, Berkshire RG11 1HF

National Chrysanthemum Society
H. B. Locke, 2 Lucas House, Craven Road,
Rugby, Warwickshire

National Council for the Conservation of Plants and Gardens
c/o Wisley Garden, Nr Woking, Surrey
GU23 6QB

National Dahlia Society
L. F. White, 'Hodellcroftys', 9a High Street,
Kingsthorpe, Northampton NN2 6QF

National Viola and Pansy Society
E. Hazleton, 16 George Street, Handsworth,
Birmingham B21 0EG

Northern Horticultural Society
Harlow Car Gardens, Crag Lane, Harrogate,
North Yorks HG3 1QB

The Royal Horticultural Society
80 Vincent Square, London SW1 2PE

The Royal Horticultural Society of Ireland
Thomas Prior House, Merrion Road,
Dublin 4, Eire

The Royal National Rose Society
Chiswell Green, St Albans, Herts. AL2 3NR

Variegated Plant Group of the Hardy Plant Society
Stephen Tassler, 'Woodlands', off Gravel Path,
Berkhamstead, Herts. HP4 2PF

SELECTED READING

Bean, W. J. *Trees and Shrubs Hardy in the British Isles Vols 1-4*, John Murray, 1976-88

Berrisford, Judith M. *Gardening on Lime*, Faber, 1963

Chatto, Beth. *The Damp Garden*, Dent 1982

Chatto, Beth. *The Dry Garden*, Dent 1981

Clausen, Ruth Rogers & Ekstrom, Nicholas H. *Perennials for American Gardens*, Random House, 1989

Crane, Howard Camp. *Gardening on Clay*, Collingridge, 1963

Crowe, Sylvia. *Garden Design*, Country Life, 1958

Fish, Margery. *Gardening in Shade*, Collingridge, 1963

Gorer, Richard. *Living Tradition in the Garden*, David & Charles, 1974

Harper, Pamela & McGourty, Frederick. *Perennials*, HP Books, 1985

Hellyer, Arthur. *The Amateur Gardener*, Collingridge, 1972

Hobhouse, Penelope. *Colour in Your Garden*, Collins, 1985

Hobhouse, Penelope. *Gertrude Jekyll on Gardening*, Collins, 1982

Hobhouse, Penelope. *Private Gardens of England*, Weidenfeld & Nicolson, 1986

Jeckyll, Gertrude. *Colour Schemes for the Flower Garden*, Country Life

Jekyll, Gertrude. *Wood and Garden*, Longman, 1899

Keen, Mary. *The Garden Border Book*, Viking, 1987

Lane-Fox, Robin. *Better Gardening*, R & L, 1982

Lloyd, Christopher. *The Mixed Border*, Collingridge, 1957

Lloyd, Christopher. *The Well-Chosen Garden*, Elm Tree Books, 1984

Lloyd Christopher. *The Well-Tempered Garden*, Viking, 1985

McGourty, Frederick. *The Perennial Gardener*, Houghton Miflin, 1989

Page, Russell. *The Education of a Gardener*, Collins, 1983

Perry, Frances. *Border Plants*, Collins, 1957

Philip, Chris. *The Plant Finder*, Headmain, 1987

Rice, Graham. *Plants for Problem Places*, Christopher Helm & Timberpress

Robinson, William. *The English Flower Garden*, John Murray 15th ed., 1933

Roper, Lanning. *Hardy Herbaceous Plants*, Penguin, 1961

Scott-James, Anne. *The Best Plants For Your Garden*, Conran Octopus, 1988

Thomas, Graham Stuart. *Perennial Plants*, Dent, 1982

Wilder, Louise Beebe. *My Garden*, Doubleday, 1932

INDEX

ACKNOWLEDGEMENTS

This book has been put together by a team. Garden writers need good gardens to write about. The standard of excellence set by the National Trust makes it a pleasure to study and describe the techniques used by their skilled Head Gardeners. It is to the latter that I wish to dedicate this book. I wish to thank Helen Sudell, Bibi Slimak and Elizabeth Harrison-Hall at Pavilion for all their hard work and, as usual, Penny David for first reading through the manuscript with her editor's eye for mistakes and omissions and helping me organise the book into a logical sequence. Tony Lord has corrected the copy for changes in botanical nomenclature. Garden photography improves all the time; I must thank all those photographers who have allowed us to use their superlative pictures. Without the designer, James Lawrence, all these other efforts might still not have made the book beautiful.

Penelope Hobhouse

PICTURE ACKNOWLEDGEMENTS

The publishers wish to thank The National Trust and The National Trust for Scotland for their kind permission to reproduce the majority of photographs in this book. Thanks also to the following photographers for their permission to reproduce the photographs listed below:

Heather Angel: pp. 16, 23, 38, 63, 89 (and both jacket shots); **Eric Crichton**: p. 18; **Andrew Lawson**: pp. 36, 51, 77. 78, 79; **Tony Lord**: pp. 7, 20, 22, 35, 57, 58, 64, 80, 81, 85, 87; **Tania Midgeley**: pp. 26, 54; **Lyndon Miller**: p. 47; **Hugh Palmer**: p. 68; **Cressida Pemberton Piggot**: pp. 27, 39, 71.

The border plans were illustrated by **Lorraine Harrison**, and the practical drawings were illustrated by **Vana Haggerty**.